MW01243565

It's More To Me, Than What You See

Revealing the Mask

by

Tequila L. Carter

Copyright Page

It's More to Me, Than What You See
by Tequila L. Carter

Scripture quotations are taken from the King James Version

Table of Contents

Dedication

This book is dedicated to my childhood youth leaders Elder Rickey Bussell and Tracye Bussell. Thanks so much for training the young people in the right direction. The trips, bible studies, lectures, and hard work doesn't go unnoticed. Love you dearly.

God is not unjust; he will not forget your work and the love you have shown him as you have helped his people and continue to help them.

-Hebrews 6:10

Acknowledgements

I would like to thank the following people who inspired me through my difficult seasons:

I would first like to thank my heavenly father who inspired me to write this book. He made me the woman I am becoming today and I am so grateful for his guidance and interventions. God thanks for catching every tear I cried and having my best interest in mind. There were so many days when I did not understand your path to my destiny but I value each lesson I learned. Thanks for never leaving me nor forsaking me when others did. Thanks for healing my wounds and making me a blessing to the body of Christ. I am so grateful for a risen savior Jesus Christ who gave himself away for my sins. I thank you for your teachings and your unfailing love. Thanks for sending me the Holy Spirit to comfort, guide, and instruct me. I love you more than words can every express. You make suffering easy when I learned of your work on the cross. I also would like to thank my parents Claude and Francis Carter and my grandmother Katie Springfield who are supportive of all my dreams. My grandfather Elder James Jackson. I acknowledge Citadel of Deliverance, True Vine Church of God in Christ and Lakeview Church of God in Christ for allowing me to use my gifts in the ministry. Special thanks to Elder Jesse Lipford, Mother Ernestine Lipford, Dianna and Willie Brooks, Barbara Prewitt, Elder George Hicks (RIP) and Leatha Hicks, Pastor Linwood Dillard, Lady Stephanie Dillard, Mother Patricia Bell, Elder and Missionary Preston, Evangelist Rochelle McIntosh (my God-mother) who I love dearly, Vickie

Houston, Herbert Houston, Dr. Vivian Wesson (such an great example to follow), Charles and Crystal Turnage, Robert and Crystal McGruder (sister, cousin, friend), Myracle Turnage (my God-daughter), Roshunda Mckinney, Terry Ford, Pastor and Missionary Hilliard, Pastor Michael Stevenson and Co-Pastor Reneice Stevenson (FVC Family) , I really wouldn't have made it if you did not allow the Lord to use you two. Thanks for your prayers, support, and fellowship. Redeem Ministry (My Prayer Circle), Dr. Peggy Harris, Evangelist Dixie Stokes, The Gatewood Family, Elder Carl Sanders and Lady Sanders, Missionary Gwendolyn Simmons, Elder Robert Simmons, Mother Louise Owens, Sister Yvette Owens, Mother Odessa Turnage, Elizabeth Kennon, Shannon Mitchell, Teen Lipford, Evangelist Dorothy Seawood, My aunties: Dorothy Wallace and Mildred Rudd, Uncle Chester, and my little brother Mario Carter, Elder Carl (Ruth) Sanders (Thanks so much for supporting me since my Sunshine Band Days), and Missionary Ardelia Collins.

Our Deepest Fear

"Our deepest fear is not that we are inadequate. Our deepest fear is that we are powerful beyond measure. It is our light, not our darkness that most frightens us. We ask ourselves, Who am I to be brilliant, gorgeous, talented, fabulous? Actually, who are you not to be? You are a child of God. Your playing small does not serve the world. There is nothing enlightened about shrinking so that other people won't feel insecure around you. We are all meant to shine, as children do. We were born to make manifest the glory of God that is within us. It is not just in some of us; it is in everyone. And as we let our own light shine, we unconsciously give other people permission to do the same. As we are liberated from our own fear, our presence automatically liberates others."

-Marianne Williamson

Foreword

There's an old saying: "don't judge a book by its cover" (unknown author). This phrase simply means you shouldn't prejudge the worth or value of something by its outward appearance alone.

We live in a visual society. Everything we learn to like, value, or strive for comes through and from what we see. Society has taught us if it doesn't look good, it must not be good. If it doesn't look like it's going to be successful, it's not worth spending time and energy on. If they don't look like they are going anywhere, drop them and find someone else.

If he or she doesn't have the look...

If he or she doesn't appear to be going anywhere in life (just by looking at them)...

(Let's get personal) If it looks like I will have to work too hard for it...

If it looks like I will have to put forth effort, discipline myself to stick with it...

If it looks like I won't reap the benefits from it right off...

If it looks like I won't get a quick return...sadly the mindset is often IT'S NOT WORTH IT!

We live in a "microwave" type society. If I can't find the value in you within the first 10 minutes, I move on to my next option. There are so many people who have counted you out. So many people who lost faith in you. So many people said you would never be anything. So many who said you would never amount to anything. So many who plotted to destroy you. So many who talked negatively about you to others. So many who painted a negative picture about you to others. And truth be told, some of us counted ourselves out!

Many of us have felt like and succumbed to when it seems like what I am doing is not getting me anywhere, I give up. When I have failed at this same thing so many times in the past, I get discouraged and toss it to the side.

When others tell me I will never be able to achieve it, somehow that negativity settles into my spirit and I am defeated before I even start. When I thought I was too old to do something different, I settled for living a "that will do" life. When I thought I would always be stuck under that generational curse, I chose not to strive for more. But, author Tequila L. Carter reminds us, "It's More To Me Than What You See!" There is so much more to you than people really see. Carter calls our attention and focus to the One who created us and knows the plan He has for our life. Our hearts and minds are turned to God's love for us and seeing Him in every aspect of our life. She confronts personal struggles we are all familiar with and puts them face to face with the Word of God. Through this book, we are re-focused, revived, and reassured that God was very intentional when he created "you."

I pray that every reader of this book comes to know their purpose and begins to walk in it despite what others have said. Every challenge, every obstacle that you have faced has made you the person you are today. It's time to pull off the labels from others and live the life God intended for you to live. I pray that every hindrance be destroyed in your life. I pray that you find the courage to speak God's Word over your life. You will succeed. You will not be defeated. You are more than a conqueror. You are victorious. Despite what has happened in the past. Despite how things may have looked before. Despite what they said about you. It's More To Me Than What You See!!!

Co Pastor Reniece Stevenson

Introduction

But the Lord said to Samuel, "Don't judge by his appearance or height, for I have rejected him. The Lord doesn't make decisions the way you do! People judge by outward appearance, but the Lord looks at a person's thoughts and intentions."

I Samuel 16:7 NLT

A local church hosted a nationwide Women's Conference at an auditorium which seated approximately 500 people. The conference host had a hidden agenda therefore she intentionally refused to announce the keynote speaker to the audience. A reserved woman arrived to the conference dressed casually who seemed very apprehensive as though she was about to encounter the biggest event of her life. She wasn't your typical evangelist, motivational speaker, or revivalist. She didn't have a well-known last name or in a high social class. Her parents were not pastors or great leaders that were well-known throughout the community. She wasn't known for her accomplishments and achievements in life. Her photo wasn't printed in magazines or the newspapers. Due to her demeanor, age, and gender many people overlooked her. The hostile ushers sat her in the back of the auditorium without any questions. People gave her cold looks as if she didn't belong there. In their minds, they felt superior to her. When the conference host announced the speaker of the hour the lady who sat at the back of the auditorium stood up and approached her way to the podium. As she walked toward the stage, there were many whispers in the audience.

Many were disappointed because they paid to hear someone popular within Christianity, someone with a nationwide broadcast on the Word network or TBN. As she continued to walk towards the stage, people were beginning to pack their belongings to leave the conference. The audience without any chance assumed this little lady wasn't fit enough to speak into their lives. They questioned how a woman casually dressed to a church function could be saved and Holy Ghost filled. Due to her age, they assumed her life experiences were limited for ministry. When the 5'2, thirty year old, dressed down, keynote speaker arrived to the podium she boldly pronounced, "It is More to Me, than What You See." Her voice was clear, crisp, and extremely persuasive. That statement was so captivating the audience gave her their complete attention. She explained to the audience that she had courageously been through the fight of her life. She gave her personal testimony about God's deliverance from depression and suicide. This woman was able to speak to women from all walks of life. She had been unemployed for several years, overcame much hurt in her life, and felt worthless and inadequate for many years. She purposely wore casual clothes so people can grasp the concept on God's principle on judging others by their physical appearance. She fiercely asked the audience to make a vow not to treat anyone less than they wanted to be treated. She told the audience how she was treated as she walked into the Conference. She endured much cruel treatment towards people who thought they had everything together. It wasn't a dry eye within the audience. Many women were delivered from rejection, their past, and several souls were added to the kingdom after she delivered her message. At the end of the conference, women were motivated to fulfill their purpose in life. And, they vowed to never look down on anyone because you never know who you're entertaining. ***Do not forget to entertain strangers, for by so doing some people have entertained angels without knowing it. Hebrews 13:2 NIV***

This isn't a true story but I wonder how many times such as this scenario people have overlooked someone because they were judging them by how they looked at a particular moment. They looked at the person's tangible characteristics such as their race, weight, height, or even their circumstances and assumed they were inadequate. Due to this prejudiced attitude, many people can not see the potential of greatness which is waiting to be discovered within their own reach. People often make the mistake of allowing others' perception to form a false reality of their own destinies. Society places a great responsibility on people to be a certain way and if they do not fit into the world's little box negative feelings arrive from within. People are left feeling unloved, rejected, depressed, averaged, and inadequate. Sadly, these misconceptions have crept into the body of Christ where people believe you have to look a certain way or have an upper class social status for you to be used by God. This attitude will cause people to conform to their environment and create chaos among believers in the church because we would rather mimic others than to become the person God has called us to be. I am aware that I have been called into the office of evangelism not necessarily to gain a title but to spread the Gospel of Jesus Christ across this nation. There are many women in this office that I admire but I would never want to mimic their style or method to reach the lost. God gave me techniques to reach people and it is my endeavor to stay within my lane. I do not allow people to tell me I have to perform a certain way in order for me to be anointed. I have confidence that God has called me the way I am. If believers are unaware of who they are it will always cause strife and division among each other. This is the reason it is extremely important for Christians to have a healthy self-esteem about themselves through their faith to Jesus Christ. We should have a healthy evaluation of ourselves. We are not better or worse than anyone else. *As God's messenger, I give each of you this warning: Be honest in your estimate of yourselves, measuring your value by how much faith God has given you. Romans 12: 3 NLV* Paul warns believers not to be self-conceited where we think we are better than others. He also warns us not to lean upon our own wisdom because everything we are and know comes from God. We are not to fight with each other for positions and things. God gives us one commandment to experience success in ministry and life. *But seek first his kingdom and his righteousness, and all these things will be given to you as well. Matthew 6:33 NIV* If we as believers would believe in this scripture and seek God we would become successful in all our affairs. But, we tear each other down, assassinate each other's character, and do unrighteous things to be in the spotlight. I have witnessed many people becoming successful but did all the wrong things to get there. People many times mistreat others just to get to the top. However, life has a strange way of creating circumstances where you will find that people you thought had everything together eventually fall apart while the people we overlooked due to our social stigmas become successful with the visions God gave them. It is so comforting to know that God does not consult anyone about our destinies. If he did, many people including myself would be counted out. For one, if God depended on man to choose who he anointed then the world will not see his glory. We would choose people from our small circles that looked a certain way. Some people would be chosen because of their high-class economic status. I remember watching my favorite sitcom, *The Game,* on this particular episode Melanie and Derwin changed memberships at church. At their new church, they sat in the VIP section in the church with other famous people. Derwin's character is a humble, famous football player who wanted to sit with everyone else in the church. Melanie stressed the point that they were paying tithes for special treatment. She even held the service up because they were running late for regular worship service. Even though this was a sitcom, it had some reality to how people view religion and church. People believe that God has categories for each member. God sent his word as an outline how we should live our lives. Regardless, how much money people pay in church, the Bible is the guideline as to how Christians should live their lives. God holds leaders accountable when we know a person isn't living his way but we excuse them because they are big tithe payers. Your economic status doesn't exempt you from living righteous according to the bible. I understand God anoints leaders to do his will on earth but it is not because of the individual's social status, parents, or anything outside of God's grace. Leaders are servants also. They should be honored and respected but God does not excuse leaders from sin. It is God's grace we are who we are and we do what we do! We need to consult God about who we appoint not our personal preferences. That's one reason we have so many appointed people not anointed people performing in the body of Christ without any power or change. They were appointed by man but not by God. I recall when God told Samuel to go to Jesse's house to anoint one of his sons king of Israel to replace Saul. The first son Samuel attempted to anoint was Eliab because he was good looking and tall. However, God rejected Eliab because God does not look on man's appearance but at the heart. God had rejected seven of Jesse's son to be anointed king of Israel. At this moment, it seemed as if God had changed his mind on Samuel. But, at the last moment Jesse told Samuel about the youngest son who at the time was attending sheep. The bible described David as ruddy, with fine appearance and handsome features. God said to Samuel arise and anoint him for he is the one. I imagined that David smelled like sheep and looked dirty from being in the field. Many people are in the fields of life some of them smell like the mess they are in. Many are dirty but God sees the potential of greatness that is in them. Even though, society would count many of them out God will use them. If you would take notice God looked at the heart of these men. The heart is the center of the total personality it holds the intuition, feelings, or emotion. The heart reveals a person's true character. We sometimes can have it together on the outside, but on the inside we are a mess just waiting to be rebuilt.

On the contrary, many people look a mess (attending to the sheep) and God has chosen them for a particular assignment. That's why we can not count people out we have no idea what's within the person's heart. Many people look ordinary but greatness is on the horizon.

God used ordinary people to do extraordinary things throughout history. *I am the Lord; that is my name! I will not give my glory to another or my praise to idols. Isaiah 42:8 NIV* Many times God can not use us because he can not trust us with his glory. We take what God has given us to bless others in the kingdom for fame. Now, I'm not saying that God will not bless you for being obedient to the call. God truly is faithful to his servants. However, we must remain focused on the reason for God using us which is to enhance God's kingdom. We shouldn't promote ourselves in ministry. I'm so tired of people who pass out business cards to get a speaking engagement. Just stay attending the sheep. God will give you an opportunity to display your gift. We are chosen for different assignments not just to preach and sing. You may be anointed to be a successful entrepreneur to bless the kingdom or start a nonprofit organization for abused women.

Many people's purpose in life will not be within the four walls of the church. God needs people in Corporate America, the Whitehouse, in the Medical field, any place where he can showcase his wondrous works. Rich people need to hear about Jesus as well as poor people. It does not matter where you are or where you have been in life. You do not have to be most popular in life either. Many times God takes an outcast or a social reject and makes something beautiful for his use. *The Spirit of the Sovereign Lord is upon me, because the Lord has appointed me to bring good news to the poor. He has sent me to comfort the brokenhearted and to announce that captives will be released and prisoners will be freed. He has sent me to tell those who mourn that the time of the Lord's favor has come, and with it, the day of God's anger against their enemies. To all who mourn in Israel, he will give beauty for ashes, joy instead of mourning, praise instead of despair. For the Lord has planted them like strong and graceful oaks for his own glory. Isaiah 61: 1-3 NLV* This particular scripture give readers details on the purpose for God anointing an individual. He has anointed him to preach good news to the poor, bind up the brokenhearted, to proclaim freedom, to give beauty for ashes, and many other things. Many times we have heard people proclaim that people are anointed due to the way they perform. However, God anoints people for a specific task. Anoint means to dedicate to the service of God. Therefore, the anointing is not a style or a certain way of performance. It simply means a person has been chosen by God to dedicate themselves to him for a specific assignment. If people don't worship God according to our style it doesn't mean they're not anointed. Have you ever heard people confess they were anointed without any evidence? They haven't helped anyone for years but they are anointed. Really! While someone may not have the tangible characteristics of the anointing (the sound or look), but they're anointed to bring change in Corporate America. We sometimes believe that poor people only need Jesus. However, people in the White

House need Jesus. Therefore, God has to anoint someone to serve in every capacity so the Gospel of Jesus can be spread abroad effectively. It's hard to convince me you are anointed but inefficient. The word inefficient means wasteful of time, energy, or materials. God holds us accountable for not being Good Stewards over the anointing he places over our lives. Anointed people don't waste prayer time gossiping about what a sister wore to church last Sunday. We don't waste our energy on clubbing on Saturday night. I can't waste my materials on supporting things that don't glorify God. People are searching for more than religion as God's people we must become everything God called us to be. God uses people so he can get the glory out of their lives. Often, people believe that you need a testimony of overcoming drugs or alcohol to be profound in the kingdom. That's a deception also. God can use anyone from diverse backgrounds to bring forth fruit. I grew up in holiness and I thank God that some experiences I was spared from. However, I would never look down on anyone. We need people from all walks of life.

During your tough and uncomfortable situations, God is creating character so once you arrive to your destination you will not allow your ego to ruin what God has design to bless the kingdom. Frequently, I have seen people in leadership allow their success to cause the greatest destruction in their lives and those around them. Not only have I seen this problem in the church but also in Corporate America. These were people who confess that God was Lord over their lives. However, they mistreated people and misused their authority. ***When the righteous are in authority, the people rejoice: but when the wicked beareth rule, the people mourn. Proverbs 29:2 KJV*** If God was Lord over their life they would realize that God did not give them authority to misuse it. He gives authority for you to bring about a change. That change begins when you accept Christ as Lord over your life. He dictates every move in your life that means you acknowledge him in every step. ***Trust in the Lord with all your heart and lean not on your own understanding; in all your ways acknowledge him, and he will make your paths straight. Proverbs 3: 5-6 NIV*** I'm not saying that every move is going to be easy. Sometimes God's will takes us through uncomfortable and hopeless situations in order for us to exercise our trust in him. We have to trust that God knows what's best for our lives. As we begin to allow God to direct us, we experience growth. This growth has nothing to do with your age or title. Do you know how many people who are in leadership positions that have not grown to maturity? They are offended easily and sometimes have a bad attitude. This will hinder God's anointing and the ministry is ineffective. God has dealt with me about serving in ministry unprepared. *If you know God has called you into ministry it is vital to prepare yourself with a prayer life, fasting, and studying his word.* So many people have told me that God was going to use me to do a great work. However, I do not allow people to push me into ministry without sitting at the feet of Jesus and learning. I have moved before God had released me and found myself out of the will of God. God is faithful you must trust him to complete the work in you.

This book will take you on a journey to experience liberation from labels, stigmas, and the will power to overcome every obstacle in your life. I personally open my heart to share intimate life struggles that had me bound by Satan tactics. These tactics led me to feel unloved, rejected, feelings of failure, and a low self-image of self. Through God's grace, God has delivered me. No more will I be silent! Open your heart and receive all God has for you through this book. Let's begin our journey.

Chapter 1
Seeing God's Love for You

See how very much our heavenly Father loves us, for he allows us to be called his children, and we really are! But the people who belong to this world don't know God, so they don't understand that we are his children.

I John 3:1 NLT

I am Loved

When people know they are loved by someone it makes living easy. Three simple words, "I Love You", can transform the life of a damaged person and make them feel they are able to conquer anything. Love is the most powerful word in the dictionary. Yet, it is used so inconsiderately. Therefore, many people can not see the depth of God's love because their perception of love is diminished by their past. People have told us they love us but their actions were so far from their words. In the distance between words and actions, we are left feeling unloved. When we feel we are unloved it leads us feeling worthless, purposeless, and undeserving of God's promises. Thus, the first and most essential step to seeing who you are in Christ is the understanding and acceptance of God's love for you. Many people have sung the popular song, "Jesus Loves Me" while growing up in church. However, many people can not accept God's love personally. They assume God only loves people who have been perfect all their lives. In reality, there are no perfect people. They have allowed the enemy to tell them because of their sins God's love has run out. **Do not allow the enemy to tell you a lie that you are not loved by God, the Father**. God loves the homosexual, prostitute, whoremonger, rapist, hateful, and any other person engaging in sinful activities. He does not love the sin that is in them but God does love them. We are often hypocritical concerning God's forgiveness to humanity. We forget how God saved us through his grace and mercy despite how rebellious we were concerning his commandments. God has a no-child left behind policy in heaven if we **repent** of our sins he is faithful to forgive them. He would that we all return to him and not perish. *But God showed his great love for us by sending Christ to die for us while we were still sinners. Romans 5:8 NLT* God loved us before we became Christians meaning while we were yet in our mess he spared us from some consequences. That explains the depth of God's love for his children. God did not allow any Sexually Transmitted Disease to attack our bodies while we were yet singing in the choir and fornicating because he loved us. Jesus' blood covered us even though we deserved to die. That's enough to praise God! **I'm not justifying anyone who sins**. Rather, I want people to live a holy life knowing that they are loved by God. People serve God with enjoyment when they do it out of love rather than obligations. I served God many times out of fear and obligations. Often I was serving God with the wrong attitude and very frustrated within ministry. The more I understood the depth of God's love for me the more I served God with enjoyment. I also want people to be free from their past. People will make you pay for your mistakes until they feel you deserve to be forgiven but not God. *As far as the east is from the west, so far hath he removed our transgression from us Psalm 103: 12 KJV* This particular scripture simply means your past sins are forgiven and forgotten by God. How dare we allow people (who have no power to forgive sin) dictate our spiritual growth. You made a mistake many years ago and still paying for it with guilt and shame. Learn from it and move on. *So now there is no condemnation for those who belong to Christ Jesus. Romans 8:1*

Father, to All

In God's No-Child Left Behind policy, there are no people exempt from receiving his love, mercy, and grace. It does not matter if a person was an orphan or mistreated by their earthly parents God loves them. *Even if my father and mother abandon me, the Lord will hold me close. Psalm 27:10 NLT* God made room for everyone so no one would be counted out from receiving his love. God's love for us is so great we are called his children. The people who belong to this world do not recognize that we are God's children; therefore we are persecuted and torn down. However, God cares and he will avenge us within his own time. Have you ever heard someone brag about their children who were proud to be a parent of a celebrity or famous person? When we acknowledge our sins and come to Jesus we make God a proud parent. *For God so loved the world that he gave his one and only Son, that whoever believes in him shall not perish but have eternal life. John 3:16 KJV* There is no greater love than this. Our existence is based on God's gift to humanity which was Jesus Christ. It is not because we deserve it, therefore we can not receive God's love by good works. Jesus Christ is a gift to us and many people have rejected God's gift to us. God's love is totally unconditional.

Every Child Has a Gift

When God created us his love placed gifts and abilities that can only be fulfilled by knowing him. God told Jeremiah *before I formed you in the womb I knew you, before you were born I set you apart, I appointed you as a prophet to the nations (Jeremiah 1:6 NIV)* God gave Jeremiah the blue print for his life at an early age. Jeremiah was called into the office of a prophet to the nations. Jeremiah felt inadequate due to his age and his inability to speak fluently. He felt he couldn't speak with authority because people would despise his youth. Although he gave God many excuses, God used him as a prophet. Jeremiah had all these limitations but it was more to him than he imagined. When God calls us to a certain purpose he knows our limited resources. He loves us so much that he overlooks our limitation. God is limitless! Jeremiah could have allowed the people to stop his destiny but he obeyed God's voice. You shouldn't allow anyone, environment, or the negative image of yourself to define who you are. If I would have known the depth of God's love for me I wouldn't have allowed people's labels to hinder my purpose or their opinions to be my identity. God's love for you has nothing to do with you which means his love is unconditional. He loves you in spite of every evil act you have done. I know the world will make you feel like your chances have run out with God but that's not the truth. When the teachers of the law brought an adulterous woman to Jesus he restored her and demonstrated love to her. According to the law, she should have been stoned to death. There is nothing more or less you can do to make God stop or start loving you. Many times

24

people measure the love of God on how they feel or their past experiences. However, the word of God is the only way you can experience and understand the totality of God's love for us. I have looked for love in so many places and with so many people and every time I was disappointed. First of all, in our generation some people do not understand the depth of love according to the word of God. They have the dictionary love. According to the Webster dictionary, love is a strong affection for another arising out of kinship or personal ties or attraction based on sexual desires. This is the wrong kind of love and is based on feelings and conditions. *According to I Corinthians 13:4-8, love is patient, love is kind it does not envy, it does not boast, it is not proud. It is not rude, it is not self-seeking, it is not easily angered, it keeps no record of wrongs. Love does not delight in evil but rejoices with the truth. It always protects, always trusts, always hopes, and always perseveres.* There is an entire difference with the world's definition of love and God's definition. You can never base God's love for us on conditions. God's love for you has not changed because you are experiencing tough times. Many times when we experience a crisis we start thinking God has changed his mind about us. This is not true. *But the Lord's plans stand firm forever; his intentions can never be shaken. Psalm 33:11 NLT* He is a consistent God and not like people. He has not changed his mind about you just because you have failed or you are experiencing hardship. Get up!!! God wants to show his love, mercy, and compassion to you through your situations.

The Sacrifice of Love

Love makes sacrifices! Jesus made sacrifices for us and not himself. Jesus gave all that he had. Not only did Jesus give up his life but he chose to give up riches that we might be rich. *You know how full of love and kindness our Lord Jesus Christ was. Though he was very rich, yet for your sakes he became poor, so that by his poverty he could make you rich. 2Corinthians 8:9 NLT* This is not just talking about monetary but his heavenly place. He left heaven to come to earth to reach us. That's how much you are loved. Jesus gave up something precious that he might gain us living with him eternally. Now, that's love. He did not just give up something that was little value to him. If you really want to know if someone loves you look at their sacrifices. Many times people look for love and really do not know how love looks. Is that person giving you something that will hurt them to give you? Or give you something they wanted. Sometimes people will give you things that have low value to them which doesn't require many sacrifices. It wouldn't require a man much to take you out to dinner every now and then. But, if you would ask him about a real commitment you would probably find out how that man really feels about you. A commitment would require that man to forsake all and be with you. Do you think you are loved? Many times we are trying to get people to love us who can not really see us. I wanted love so bad from people that I would change who I was in order to get them to love me. Not knowing that it was impossible to be loved by someone who couldn't see my greatness in spite of my flaws, weaknesses, and disappointments. Many times because I did not know who I was people would prey on my weaknesses. They knew I was hurting which caused me to be vulnerable. Therefore, whatever they wanted me to be that's who I became. On jobs, I would let people use me and never spoke up for myself. In relationships and friendships, I would allow people to walk all over me as if I was a doormat. Often, especially in platonic relationships I would be hurt because I treated that relationship as if it was more than what it was. I take some responsibility for that. However, I felt that the other parties never took responsibility that I was misled. Therefore, I felt betrayed by that. I felt that people knew I was looking for love and preyed on that particular vulnerability. My heart was broken and I experienced great pain. However, during that time I would feel God's love in great capacity. I felt that he was nearer to me in my painful moments. *The Lord is close to the brokenhearted; he rescues those who are crushed in spirit. Psalm 34:18* Sometimes we believe when people do not love us there is something wrong with us. This is not true. I had to accept the love sacrifice of Jesus Christ. This man had done so much for me to prove his love and sometimes I felt that wasn't enough. I needed that human touch and was disappointed every time. But, when I fell in love with Jesus I was no longer looking for love but looking to love someone as Jesus loved me.

God Loves Me In spite of My Past

Someone may be reading this book and yet believe their past overshadows God's ability to use or love them. However, in the bible there was a prostitute by the name of Rahab who hid three Hebrews spies. See Joshua Chapter 2 It was Rahab's

27

faith that made her believe that God was real. She therefore saved herself and family when Jericho fell. Paul quoted her name when he discussed faith. *It was by faith that Rahab the prostitute did not die with all the others in her city who refused to obey God. Hebrews 11:31 NLT* Although this woman was a harlot (prostitute), her name was quoted throughout the bible. I told you it is more to you than people can see. God's love protected Rahab even though she did not deserve it. Receiving God's love is simple according to the scriptures. God only asks that we acknowledge our faults to him. *But if we confess our sins to him, he is faithful and just to forgive us and to cleanse us from every wrong. I John 1:9 NLT* I do not care what you have done God's love will cover you. He immediately restores us back to himself through Jesus Christ. Jesus Christ is the only way to God. So many times people confess that they want to be like Christ but they are not telling the truth. We can not forgive sins but we can help restore our sisters or brothers back to God. Christians must be careful with condemning and not restoring people back to God. *Dear brothers and sisters, if another Christian is overcome by some sin, you who are godly should gently and humbly help that person back onto the right path. Galatians 6:1 NLT* If you are claiming to be a Christian restoring people that have fallen is a part of your duty. We often kill people because of one mistake. We forget about the times they came to church looking for help. If we would allow God to restore that person they would probably become more powerful Christians. Instead, we boast about how we've never experienced the sin others have. This is why walking in love is so important.

28

Love forgives! Love restores! Love forgets! *Hatred stirs up quarrels, but love covers all offenses. Proverbs 10:12 NLT* Why do we run and tell what others have done? We hinder a lot of God's work with **GOSSIP**. Half of the things we hear have been twisted by four different people before the truth actually comes out. When we gossip about what others have done we are not walking in God's love. It has been done to me. It does not feel good when restoration needs to be shown and we yet criticize and tear others down. Everyone in ministry should walk in integrity and that is my aim. However, we must realize even anointed people are just flesh. Sometimes we say the wrong things and do the wrongs things. We have not arrived yet either. God dealt with me about gossiping about things I have seen with my own eyes. God asked me one day have you prayed for that particular individual or confronted that person in love about their sin? (When we confront in love, people shouldn't feel worst about their sin they should feel restored) My response was no. God told me to close my mouth and pray for that person. I noticed when I started praying for that individual God helped me and the other party. So many times I have walked in error. Even after I repented, people in the church were still talking about things I had done. According to them, I shouldn't have been praising God because I had done something out of the will of God. It was hard to escape my past when I was continually reminded of it. I had to depend on God's love for me and move on to my destination. All I could do is repent and turn from that way. I couldn't allow that sin to take me further out of the will of God just because people weren't willing to forgive me. In my prayer time, I asked

God to help me with my weaknesses and God helped me. In this time alone, you do not have to hide anything from God. You can take the church mask off. I want people to be free therefore it's time to stop pretending like we're free and actually experience freedom. We must take the mask off to experience freedom. People sometimes can not repent because we will judge them before they ask for forgiveness. He already knows everything you have done and the thoughts that are far off. Remember we are trying to be set free and the truth is the only thing that will set us free. There is always something or someone to remind us why we FEEL we do not deserve God's love. I emphasize the word "FEEL" because love is not based on the way we feel. Women who accept abuse from a man "FEELS" that he beats her because he loves her so much. Feelings are very deceptive. The enemy plays with our feelings because he knows that God loves us in spite of our past. It may be something we've done or something done to us in our past. Regardless, we must release the past. It is a difficult process when people from our past keep reminding us who we were before our Christ days. Sometimes the failures we've had while we claim to be Christians can be a hindrance. As an upcoming ministry leader, I struggled to do the will of God because of my past. I felt unworthy to do God's will because I was often reminded of my past. The past would not let me go and I was bound by it. I couldn't be forgiven and walked in unforgiveness toward people who offended me. Many of my visions for my life were distorted because my past stood dead in my face. My past changed my perception of myself. I was ashamed! My life was filled with the "I can't(s)". I felt I can't get married because of my past. I can't minister because of my past. I can't be delivered because of my past. My business can't be restored because of my past. But, thanks are unto God who has delivered me from my past. First, God reminded me that he loved me in spite of every wrong decision I've ever made. When I realized God loved me it did not matter how many people knew what I had done. As matter of fact, since people were already talking about what I had done, I decided to tell my story myself so God could get the glory. When God delivered me from my past he took away the shame. We sometimes punish ourselves with negative emotions such as guilt, unforgiveness to self, unforgiveness to others, and shame. Jesus paid the price why should I pay the price with condemnation. When we ask God for forgiveness through Jesus Christ we do not have to pay for atonement. They did that in the Old Testament. All I have to do is repent from the heart and confess I am saved. There are two types of people that suffer from their past. (1) People who are ashamed because they committed a sinful act. (2) People who are ashamed because a sinful act was committed to them. Regardless, if we were the victim or perpetrator we have to let it go to receive freedom. There are many people in the body of Christ who have been molested and raped in their past and questioned why God would allow this to happen if he loved them. We do not deal with these issues within the church because many are too embarrassed to tell. Molestation is something that will keep a person ashamed if they are not delivered. There are men and women battling with sexual perversion because of their past. Some struggle with homosexuality due to them being molested by a person of the same sex. You may have been molested by a close family member or friend and felt betrayed. This incident does not mean you should think low about yourself and feel unloved by God. It was the lust of the person that did this to you. You are not the blame! However, you are yet loved and God is able to heal your wound. It is a tough pill to swallow but you have to forgive your offender. FORGIVENESS IS NOT FOR THE OFFENDER BUT IT IS FOR YOU. God will deal with your offender and hopefully they will repent. Anger, resentment, and bitterness will rob you from your true deliverance. You will not be free from your past with unforgiveness. You are not alone on this! Someone has experienced being molested or raped by a close relative or friend. I guarantee there are many people within our churches that we sit on the same pew with who have been molested. You must know that molestation did not just happen in our generation but since the beginning of time. There was a virgin by the name of Tamar who was molested by her brother Amnon in the bible. She did not deserve it and wasn't asking for it. Her brother took her virginity. *David's son Absalom had a beautiful sister named Tamar. And Amnon, her half brother, fell desperately in love with her. Amnon became so obsessed with Tamar that he became ill. She was a virgin, and it seemed impossible that he could ever fulfill his love for her. Now Amnon had a very crafty friend his cousin Jonadab. He was the son of David's brother Shimea. One day Jonadab said to Amnon, "What's the trouble? Why should the son of a king look so dejected morning after morning?" So Amnon told him, I am in love with Tamar, Absalom's sister." "Well," Jonadab said,*

"I'll tell you what to do. Go back to bed and pretend you are sick. When your father comes to see you, ask him to let Tamar come and prepare some food for you. Tell him you'll feel better if she feeds you." So Amnon pretended to be sick. And when the king came to see him, Amnon asked him, "Please let Tamar come to take care of me and cook something for me to eat." So David agreed and sent Tamar to Amnon's house to prepare some food for him. When Tamar arrived at Amnon's house, she went to the room where he was lying down so he could watch her mix some dough. Then she baked some special bread for him. But when she set the serving tray before him, he refused to eat. "Everyone get out of here," Amnon told his servants. So they all left. Then he said to Tamar, "Now bring the food into my bedroom and feed it to me here." So Tamar took it to him. But as she was feeding him, he grabbed her and demanded, "Come to bed with me, my darling sister." "No, my brother!" she cried. "Don't be foolish! Don't do this to me! You know what a serious crime it is to do such a thing in Israel. Where could I go in my shame? And, you would be called one of the greatest fools in Israel. Please, just speak to the king about it, and he will let you marry me."

But, Amnon wouldn't listen to her, and since he was stronger than she was, he raped her. Then suddenly Amnon's love turned to hate, and he hated her even more than he had loved her!" "Get out of here!" he snarled at her. "No, no!" Tamar cried. "To reject me now is a greater wrong than what you have already done to me." But Amnon wouldn't listen to her. He shouted for his servant and demanded, "Throw this woman out, and lock the door behind her!" So the

servant put her out. She was wearing a long, beautiful robe, as was the custom

in those days for the king's virgin daughters. But now Tamar tore her robe and

put ashes on her head. And then, with her face in her hands, she went away

crying. 2 Samuel 13:1-19

Notice the bible says her brother was so ill, that he fell sick for his sister Tamar. He had the issue not her. She did not seduce him, dress inappropriately, or manipulate him. Amnon allowed his friend to influence him to sin against his own sister. He reminded Amnon of his social status which was the king's son. So many times people believe because of their "titles" they have the ability to do whatever they want. Many people in authority prey on the weak because they think they are getting by. They are not getting by and God will give their victims justice. Amnon knew Tamar loved him as a brother and he took advantage of the situation. He pretended to be weak in order to display his strength on Tamar. Due to her character, she begged him to marry her so she wouldn't be filled with shame. However, Amnon raped her and afterwards hated her. Amnon hated her even though she hadn't done anything wrong. He was in fault. Amnon left Tamar's life in brokenness. Tamar was ashamed about her past and she never got passed it. In those days, women did not have a voice to cry out for help. However, we do! You do not have to be like Tamar and remain silent and hurt. You can allow this wound to bring you into your full potential and help other people dealing with the same issues. Betrayal from a family member or someone we trusted can sometimes leave us feeling lonely, unloved, ashamed, and depressed. But, we bind the power of Satan and command him to release us from our past. It does not matter if you were like Tamar and was raped or if you had consensual sex with someone who later hates you. God still loves you and you do not have to use your body because you feel unloved. You are loved and God will help you through this situation. He will heal you from your past. You must also know that you are not alone in this situation. There are many people that have dealt with rape and molestation. It is a wound that can not be ignored rather it must be healed from the root. If not it will definitely show up in other areas of your life. The number one problem with people being molested and raped is promiscuity. If you are struggling to forgive please confess this prayer daily:

<u>Prayer to God</u>

Father, we thank you for your love shown toward us through Jesus Christ.
We ask you to forgive us of all unrighteousness.
Help us to forgive those who have wounded us.
Help us to forgive ourselves who we have wounded.
Heal our emotional and spiritual wounds.
Help us to walk in love and restore people from our families, churches, work places, and anyone who need to be restored.
God, help us not to judge others and condemn others.
Help us to release our past.
Use us for your glory to build your kingdom.
Amen

God's Character

We were created in God's image. ***So God created people in his own image; God patterned them after himself; male and female he created them. Genesis Chapter 1:27 NLT*** How many times have you heard that preached in a sermon? How would we know God's image if we never study his word? This is why people have a misconception about themselves and about God. We need to understand that God is eternal which means he has no beginning or ending. *Before the mountains were created, before you made the earth and the world, you are God, without beginning or end. Psalm 90:2 NLT* That's the highest level of security we as people can have, everything around us may be shaken but God will always be around. Different people may be placed in government, companies diminished, people leave us, but God is always there. I love God so much because he was there all the time. In the midst of my struggles, he remained faithful. *The unfailing love of the Lord never ends! By his mercies we have been kept from complete destruction. Great is his faithfulness; his mercies begin afresh each day. Lamentations 3:22* Once people understand that concept there will be so much comfort. I remember when I was going through God shifting people out of my life. I was so lonely at the time but afraid to allow new people into my life because I was afraid they would leave me also. But, God reminded me that he was an everlasting God. He would never leave me. First of all, we know that God loves us. If he loves us then we know that every bad experience God will make it good. *And we know that God causes everything to work together for the good of those who love God and are called according to his purpose for them. Romans 8:28 NLT* If you are reading this book I believe you love God and are called according to his purpose. Think about every bad situation in your life. Now see it through God's eyes and begin to praise him for the good that is coming your way. He is unchangeable. *But you are always the same; your years never end. Psalm 102:27 NLT* God does not change in his character. The older I get the more I notice that people change. People that I knew ten years ago are not the same today as they were. Some for the good and some for the worse. People will say they are with you but when you hit rock bottom you are not able to find them. People will say they will help you until helping you takes them out their comfort zone. But, God is nothing like people. There is nobody greater than him. I am so grateful that God does not change with the seasons.

My Story of God's Love

I can relate to this chapter so much because at one time in my life I felt unloved by God. I have questioned God as to why he would allow me to go through the most embarrassing situations. Often, I have felt like crawling under a rock and not returning to existence. I have felt so inadequate and abused by life that I couldn't see God using me. I was blinded by Satan and believed that God was punishing me for some evil I had done. I measured the love of God with my circumstances and the negative feelings toward myself. I said to myself if God loved me then he wouldn't have allowed me to suffer. This was a big misconception on my part. One day I was sitting in church and God gave me *Isaiah 61:7 NLT Instead of shame and dishonor, you will inherit a double portion of prosperity and everlasting joy.* I went through things and people knew about my situations everywhere I went. I did not have private afflictions. I was publicly going through my situations. Many times God allows us to be embarrassed so he can put us on display. He creates a situation so he can get the glory out of it. I believe God has a unique sense of humor. He loves when people count us out so he can show his capabilities. Whenever I face those life situations that make me feel hopeless I remind myself that I am loved by God. This attitude kept me pursuing my dreams. It kept me waking up in the morning looking for a way out of my situation. I do not care who does not love me knowing that God loves me eases the pain of rejection of others. God's love is not based on conditions. So, the next time the car falls apart do not question God's love for you. It is called life. We live in a falling world. In life, we sometimes experience things that can be detrimental to us. This does not mean God is angry and his love has changed. Then I wasn't mature enough to understand the real love of God. Therefore, Satan deceived me many times. God loves us but the Devil is always at war with what God loves. This is the reason we experience pain. We are so special that God and the Devil are at war for our souls. The enemy is mad because some of us have turned from our wicked ways and God is winning. We should never blame God for our pain. *I Peter 5:8 NLT Be careful! Watch out for attacks from the Devil, your great enemy. He prowls around like a roaring lion, looking for some victim to devour.* According to this scripture, we all have our own personal adversary. The scripture clearly makes it personal by stating (YOUR ENEMY). My enemy may not be your enemy. If I struggle with addiction to alcohol you're not better if you struggle with addiction to cigarettes. It's all an addiction. That's why we experience different things in life. I couldn't see that God loved me so much when I felt like giving up he sent me a prophetic word to give me hope. He wanted me to know that he was with me. Regardless what I faced, God was there all the time. People would misjudge me because I faced difficult situations. I had some friends like Job which compared my spiritual walk with my circumstances. They had no idea the intensity of my pain. They examined my life and made false accusations because I was going through my time of suffering. They were unaware that God's love would lift me up one day. My suffering seasons was my preparation seasons. I guarantee if someone has a great destiny they would have as story for God's glory. All our stories are different. God loves diversity in his kingdom. Therefore, we should never minimize someone because their story is not our story. Some women have children outside of marriage and may experience ridicule from other Christians. However, if we tell the truth it is by the grace of God that many of us do not have children out of wedlock. We should embrace that young mother and give her agape love. The enemy uses different bait to make us fall into damnation. When we grasp that idea into our minds we wouldn't be so judgmental one to another. I may not have struggled with drugs and alcohol but the enemy used other bait for me like unforgiveness, hatred, bitterness, and lust. However, there is a correlation with a drug addict and me. The root of it is called pain. *The scarifies of God are a broken spirit: a broken and a contrite heart, O God, thou will not despise. Psalms 51:17KJV*   The word contrite in this text means crushing. Someone reading this book may ask, "How can God allow me to be crushed if he loves me?" The word crush means to squeeze or force by pressure so as to alter or destroy structure. Crushing really hurts. It is not a simple hit but rather being smashed, beaten with severe pain which literally destroys our structure. Job had a crushing encounter. Although he was faithful to God, he was tempted with tragedy. ***You formed me with your hands, you made me, and yet you completely destroy me. Job 10: 8*** Sometimes what God allows feels as if he is trying to destroy us. God only allows pain to change us. He wants the anointing to come forth and it will only come if you have been crushed. After being crushed, you have to draw closer to God. If we do not draw closer to God the enemy will use that pain as bait for temptation. Pain will cause you to do something out the will of God. Have you ever sat down with someone (not all cases) that deals with sexual immorality? The majority of the time they have been sexually abused or experienced a devastating hurt from someone close to them. The enemy uses this wound to destroy themselves. Why? Because they feel that no one loves them and they feel worthless and they will do anything to ease this pain. The lies from the enemy will keep them from pursing God. Satan will deceive people into believing that God is not for them. I know because I've been there.

Before I embraced the love of God, I looked for love in all the wrong places. I would look for love in my career, relationships, and friends. Each time I was left feeling disappointed. After failure after failure, failed relationships, and failed friendships I finally realized that true fulfillment comes from above only. Anything outside of God is temporary. God's love is everlasting and unfailing. I experienced great hurts trying to pursue people who weren't designed for my life.

I tried my best to make them fit like a missing puzzle piece. Due to them not fitting, my soul was left fragmented. I had a piece of a career, a piece of a relationship, and a piece of friends. I was tired and I wanted "P-E-A-C-E" and not a "P-I-E-C-E" of anything anymore. I asked God to make me whole. My healing process was the most difficult process I experienced. I lost absolutely everything and a lot of people gave up on me. I take responsibility some was my fault. However, people who labeled themselves as "Christians" weren't restoring me. People knew that I was hurting and they did me just like they did Jesus. Instead of water they gave me vinegar. David said in Psalm 69:19-21 NLT ***You know the insults I endure the humiliation and disgrace. You have seen all my enemies and know what they have said. Their insults have broken my heart, and I am in despair. If only one person would show some pity; if only one would turn and comfort me. But instead, they give me poison for food; they offer me sour wine to satisfy my thirst.***

David said if only one person would show some pity! Sometimes all you need is one hug or one encouraging word. But, there comes a point in life when you will have to encourage yourself. The rejection I felt was painful, but the embarrassment was more painful. While going through my making process, it wasn't people on the outside of Christianity that did the most judging, it was people who labeled themselves as Christians. (*I'm not bashing anyone but the pain was real to me*) Instead of people being genuinely concerned about my situations, they were mostly concerned about getting into my business. I had to hear comments like,

41

"she is suffering because she did something wrong, or people do not like her because she is this horrible person." I could have taken the words better if it wasn't coming from people who called themselves Christians or people I felt were close to me. In life you will learn that familiar people can hurt you worse than strangers. I had to stop blaming others and take into account my responsibility for my own hurt. If you really want to get delivered then you have to be accountable for your actions. Even if that meant apologizing when I knew I was innocent or apologizing to people who hurt me more than words could express. As I stated earlier, I experienced betrayal from people who intentionally got close to me to use information to destroy my name and character. *It is not an enemy who taunts me I could bear that. It is not my foes who so arrogantly insult me I could have hidden from them. Instead, it is you my equal, my companion and close friend. What good fellowship we enjoyed as we walked together to the house of God. Psalm 55:12-14* My process has taught me to be careful who you share your intimate business to. I heard someone say when people attempt to get into your business respond by asking, "What will you do with the information I'm about to download to you?" Examine people's motives! Married women shouldn't tell unwise loose mouth women about what goes on in their house unless the person is saved and filled with God's spirit. You might be downloading the wrong information to an individual who secretly desires to be in your place. Yes, we are going to address many "REAL LIFE ISSUES" in this book. I've never been married but I've mistakenly downloaded the wrong information to the wrong

42

source in relationships. People with the wrong motives intentionally get close to you to destroy something in your life to get something in their life. Don't help them pray about sharing information.

People leave churches or do not come because they get hurt. But, you shouldn't allow the hurt from flawed human beings hinder you from a loving God who gave us Jesus (His only begotten son). Everyone in the church is not a hypocrite. If we be honest with ourselves we hurt people too. Sometimes we play the role of the victim when we are the perpetrator. When you are hurt it is not the time to leave but take a look at yourself. I was hurt so many times as a result I would hurt people. I wanted people to feel my pain. I was in the church, but I was looking for love in all the wrong places. But, because I wore a smile, sweet fragrance, and nice clothes people assumed I had it altogether. They didn't know behind the smile I struggled with depression and insomnia due to unresolved issues in my life. I will give in detail later on. Of course, I believe in dancing and praising God while going through my storm but they did not know my praises were keeping me sane. I would praise God to release the heaviness off me from crying myself to sleep at night. One day I became tired! I was tired of begging people to stay who wanted to leave me. I was tired of keeping people who did not want to be kept. I had to let people go. It was very painful but I knew if they stayed it was unhealthy for me. I prayed everyday that God would deliver me, not release me. After this, I had my Well Experience with Jesus. A Well Experience is when you run out of resources and you choose to drink from the water where you will never thirst again. *(John*

4:4-18 He had to go through Samaria on the way. Eventually he came to the Samaritan village of Sychar, near the parcel of ground that Jacob gave to his son Joseph. Jacob's well was there; and Jesus, tired from the long walk, sat wearily beside the well about noontime. Soon a Samaritan woman came to draw water, and Jesus said to her, "Please give me a drink." He was alone at the time because his disciples had gone into the village to buy some food. The woman was surprised, for Jews refuse to have anything to do with Samaritans. She said to Jesus, "You are a Jew, and I am a Samaritan woman. Why are you asking me for a drink?" Jesus replied, "If you only knew the gift God has for you and who I am, you would ask me, and I would give you living water." "But sir, you don't have a rope or a bucket," she said, "and this is a very deep well. Where would you get this living water? And besides, are you greater than our ancestor Jacob who gave us this well? How can you offer better water than he and his sons and his cattle enjoyed?" Jesus replied, "People soon become thirsty again after drinking this water. But the water I give them takes away thirst altogether. It becomes a perpetual spring within them, giving eternal life." "Please, sir," the woman said, "give me some of that water! Then I'll never be thirsty again, and I won't have to come here to haul water." "Go and get your husband," Jesus told her. "I don't have a husband," the woman replied. Jesus said, "You're right! You don't have a husband for you have had five husbands, and you're aren't even married to the man you're living with now."

This Samaritan woman that Jesus had encountered had been in many relationships with men and her current friend was still not ordained by God. Jesus begins to teach this woman how to pursue a relationship with God by worshipping him. Worship is deeper than coming to church. Worship is the act where we show God his worth to us. She was expecting the Messiah to come one day and did not know that she was talking to the Messiah. After she left Jesus she left her water jar and went back to town to tell people about what Jesus had done for her. So many times like this Samaritan woman we are searching for Jesus because people have made it more complicated than it really is. It is so simple just call him and he will be there. *And anyone who calls on the name of the Lord will be saved. Acts 2:21* You have to realize when it is time to drop your water jar and stop thirsting after things that will not quench your thirst and come to Jesus. People, money, careers, and other things will not satisfy you in totality. Everything you need is in Jesus. I'm not saying because we have Jesus we shouldn't have people, career, and things in our lives. I am saying we shouldn't pursue these things for fulfillment. There was a time in my life that I had nothing and hit rock bottom. Although there were many times I cried, overall I had joy. This joy did not come from the world but it came from knowing Jesus. People who had careers, people, and things they desired seemed unfulfilled. I realized that if Jesus is absent from your life I do not care what you possess you will not experience real joy and peace. This only comes from knowing you are loved by God. The thief comes only to steal and kill and destroy; I have come that they may have life, and have it to the full. *John 10:10*

The only way you can resist Satan's plan is to submit God through his son Jesus.

You are deeply LOVED by God! If you're lonely, feeling undeserving, and life

has handed you a tough season abide in the shadow of God's love.

Chapter 1 Affirmation

God
Is
Love

I See Myself as Being Loved
I am Loved By the Creator of my Soul
It Does not Matter What Sin I Have Done
If I confessed it, he Has Forgiven it
I Will No Longer Feel Unloved,
Because I Know I am Loved
This Love Does not Hurt
This Love is Real
This Love Does not Cost
This Love Made Me The Way I AM
This Love Put Gifts in Me to Share With The World
I am Gifted, I am Protected, I am Secured
I am
Loved
It is More to Me than What they Can See!!

Chapter 2

Seeing Yourself as God Sees You

I praise you because I am fearfully and wonderfully made; your works are wonderful, I know that full well. Psalm 139:14 NIV

<u>Who Am I Really?</u>

We often view God as a man on the throne with a long white silky beard in fairytale land that can only be reached by planting three magical beans in a special place to grow a beanstalk large enough to reach him. But, God is closer than the hairs on our heads and he sees us like no one else can see us. Many people's perception of us is based on what they can see in the natural. Anyone that sees me knows I am a woman. They see my feminine traits and perceive that's what I am. That's what they see. However, they wouldn't know what type of woman I was until they have an in-depth conversation with me. If people do not get to know me their perception of me can be flawed. Many times people see us going through our transformations and automatically assume that our current struggles are our destination. However, we are going through a transition. A transition is a passage from one state, stage, subject, or place to another. You are passing through many tribulations and storms to become the person God sees you as. Some people go through several bad relationships before they receive the ideal husband or wife, while some people go through a season of rejection only to receive God's acceptance to a better opportunity. *It is so important that we do not allow the enemy to make us complacent with our transitional stage.* When we allow our former man to hinder our new man we are not being the person God wants us to be. *What this means is that those who become Christians become new persons. They are not the same any more, for the old life is gone. A new life has begun! 2 Corinthians 5:17 NLT* You're not the person from five years ago if Jesus has come into your life. I do not care who you were God sees you differently now. It is time now to let go of old things and people that define you by your yesterday years.

Even though I've been in church all my life, I've always struggled with insecurity and low self-image. I felt anyone could be great but me. I felt I wasn't pretty enough or smart enough to fulfill my purpose. But, God saw the best in me. I remember when I was praying in my secret closet, God revealed to me that greatness was on the inside of me. Regardless, if I felt small within my own eyes because God was in my life I was able to conquer anything. *For in him we live and move and exist. Acts 17: 28 NLT* I'm so glad God sees us beyond the way we feel about ourselves. He sees our hurts, disappointments, anger, rejections, and he still believes we are his best creation. God also sees our lives thirty years beforehand. We must remember God considered our past, present, and future before he spoke into our lives and he still sees the best in us. Before God spoke that I would become a successful entrepreneur, he knew I would be unemployed for two years. My dilemma did not change God's mind. As a matter of fact, struggling with finding a job forced me to start my own business and be responsible with my current career. God is faithful! Many times people will give up on us due to a lack of long suffering but God will always remain. *I waited patiently for the Lord to help me, and he turned to me and heard my cry. He lifted me out of the pit of despair, out of the mud and the mire. Psalm 40 1-2* God is closer to us than we believe during our difficult times. Often the enemy will lie to us and make us feel distant toward God during our transformation stage. However, God is closer to us especially when we are in the broken stages of our lives. God always sees the bigger picture. A person can be a drug addict who is overlooked by humanity but God sees a man that lost his vision for his dreams and uses drugs to drown the pain of disappointments. If that drug addict would see the potential God invested within the individual he would arise above drug addiction and became the million dollar entrepreneur God called him to be. So many times, people circumstances blind them from the way God sees them. It is so important that we lose sight on our current circumstances, other people's opinions, and our negative opinions of ourselves and grab hold unto faith for our visions. After my job loss, there were many days I had to deal with the feeling of worthlessness, inadequacy, and purposelessness. In those moments it was my visions that helped me persevere. I was unemployed but I knew I was going some where. People often said negative things to hinder me from seeing what God had spoken. I knew destiny was calling me. I would sit in my office for countless ours daydreaming about what I wanted to do with my life. I wanted to write books and become a successful entrepreneur. I wanted to travel the world preaching the gospel of Jesus

Christ. I hear many people saying that they ran from their calling. I did also by allowing people to tell me I was too young or inexperienced to pursue my calling. However, they did not know what I had been through would help people across this world. I wasn't qualified because of Tequila Carter but by Jesus Christ. People wanted me to pursue the American Dream I wanted to pursue the Kingdom Dream. Some people had good intentions and tried to help but God wouldn't allow them to. They were trying to take me off the path God called me to follow due to fear. Before I was unemployed, God gave me a dream that I was going to follow my destiny. Sometimes that destiny caused me to travel on some narrow roads. *But the gateway to life is small, and the road is narrow, and only a few ever find it. Matthew 7:14 NLT* Not everyone was following the path I was on due to fear. It was the non-traditional way, and required much faith. I was totally shocked where I received the most opposition from. It was Christians who quoted scriptures, praised God, and claimed to have faith that couldn't see me as an evangelist, entrepreneur, or author. They only saw my transitional stage. That's why we have to be careful who we share our dreams with. I refused to allow people's words to override God's word. Staying down was not my destiny! *Rejoice not against me, O mine enemy: when I fall, I shall arise; when I sit in darkness, the Lord shall be a light unto me. Micah 7:8 KJV* God saw greatness in my uprising while other people saw the failure of my past in me. It is so important that people understand the importance in not giving up in the beginning stages of our lives. Falling down sometimes does not mean you are a failure it just means you have a temporary set back. In this temporary setback, you can enjoy every moment of the time while waiting on God. People do not like to hear "wait" because they believe it means torment. However, while waiting on God you can work on becoming a better person. During my unemployment, I did everything I complained I wanted to do when I was working a 9 to 5. I complained that I did not have time to go to church. So, every opportunity I had to be in the house of God, I was there. I wanted to travel so I visited Virginia, Georgia, Texas, Louisiana, Florida, and many more states. I found joy in meeting new people from all walks of life. To make extra money, I would go to Third Street in Memphis, Tennessee to have Rummage Sales. I met the most amazing people. I remember meeting a woman named Ms. Betty, I loved talking to this woman she was funny and overcame an abusive relationship. God brought the best out of me. When I had my job, there were certain people I wouldn't talk to but God changed me through my afflictions. *It is good for me that I have been afflicted; that I might learn thy statutes. Psalm 119:71 KJV* God taught me that there are many talented people with many different abilities from all walks of life that experienced misfortune. I once asked a beggar on the street what happened during his life that caused him to be homeless and on drugs. I gave him money several times and I wanted to know why he wouldn't get a job. He explained that years ago he was a successful dentist who had a nice home, family, and was happy. He had a nervous breakdown after he was performing a routine surgery on patient and the patient died. That was the most heartbreaking story I've heard since being in Memphis, Tennessee. Many people's story does not hit the news stations. God delivered me from self-righteousness that particular day. Sit down and have a 30 minute conversation with people and you'll find the most gifted people who are allowing a temporary set back get the best of them. We must also remember not everyone on the system wants to be there. We have to stop judging and pray for people because God does not see as man sees.

Visions

Habakkuk (a prophet) saw the terrible things that were happening to the nation of Judah. The nation refused to change their sinful ways. As a prophet, Habakkuk was like many people in ministry today, the trouble of the people caused him to be sorrowful. However, Habakkuk stood on his watch to see what the Lord had to say about his dilemma. God responded by telling Habakkuk *to **write the vision and make it plain upon tables, that he may run that readeth it. For the vision is yet for an appointed time, but at the end it shall speak, and not lie: though it tarry, wait for it; because it will surely come, it will not tarry. Behold, his soul which is lifted up is not upright in him: but the just shall live by his faith. Habakkuk 2:4 KJV** God saw Habakkuk's situation differently than what he saw. It is as important as Christians that we have a vision for our lives as we work within the four walls of the church. Church should create visions so you can do God's will on Earth. It is more than shouting and praying for one another but it is mostly about having a support system to complete God's vision for your life. Visions are the ability or an instance of great perception, especially of future developments. Most people are lost due to the lack of vision for their lives. They wake up in the morning going by the day just existing. Some people go to college and choose majors without any visions for their education. I spent thousands of dollars trying to figure out what career I wanted to purse. At first I wanted to become an Optometrist until I was informed how many years it was going to take to complete the degree. Then, I wanted to pursue Business Administration. My third choice was an English major. I wanted to write. Finally, I decided to pursue Business Administration. But, I went through college years without any direction. I decided I wanted clear direction.

Destroy Low Self-Image

How do you really see yourself? Take a moment to ponder on this question. Do you see yourself doing great things or staying mediocre? In God's kingdom, there are no mediocre gifts. When we serve people and him with our gifts with the spirit of excellence we are giving God the best. He deserves to be served with the best. This is not to say that people will not have different portions of their gifts. For instance, a pastor who has a congregation of 50 members can have the spirit of excellence over their lives like a pastor with 5000 members.My colleague once told me that bigger ships do not mean we are not traveling on the same water. We are all different but we are all trying to reach the same goal which is spreading the Gospel of Jesus Christ. We are all somebody in God's kingdom we all have a gift that will bless others. Sometimes we have allowed people to reshape our image of God's creation. Since the beginning of time, we were created in God's image to do extraordinary things throughout the world. When God completed his work he complimented himself and said "It is Good." However, we have allowed our experiences and people to detour us from our original plans. The world has a view on self-esteem which is unhealthy. Our self-esteem should be based on things that are internal not on external. The world's system would argue that one has to be physically attractive, raised in a prosperous environment, and have a healthy childhood in order for that person to have a healthy self-esteem. Due to this presumption, many people without these attributes feel worthless but God says the just shall live by faith. You have to have faith in order to see it is more to you than what you look like and possess. Paul warned believers about conforming to the worldly system in Romans 12:2. We have used that scripture for music, dress codes, and behavior but not about our self-esteem. I am so happy I do not have to look like or act like a celebrity in order to feel good about myself. I do not need cosmetic surgery every month, to feel worthy of myself. You should love yourself according to God's word. He does not want us to attempt to find ourselves outside of his word. He has said something concerning each area that we can feel special too.

Physical Appearance: Psalm 139:13-15 NIV

For you created my inmost being;

You knitted me together in my mother's womb.

I praise you because I am fearfully and wonderfully made;

Your works are wonderful,

I know that full well.

My frame was not hidden from you

when I was made in the secret place,

when I was woven together in the depths of the earth.

Acceptance: I Corinthians 1:28 NLT

God chose things despised by the world, things counted as nothing at all, and used

them to bring to nothing what the world considers important, so that no one can

ever boast in the presence of God.

Success: Jeremiah 29:11 NLT

For I know the plans I have for you, "says the LORD. "They are plans for good

and not for disaster, to give you a future and a hope.

Intelligence: James 1:5 NLT

If you need wisdom if you want to know what God wants you to do ask him, and

he will gladly tell you.

Personality: Galatians 5:22-23 NLT

But when the Holy Spirit controls our lives, he will produce this kind of fruit in us: love, joy, peace, patience, kindness, goodness, faithfulness, gentleness, and self-control.

Self-Worth Psalm 100:3 NLT

Acknowledge that the Lord is God! He made us, and we are his. We are his people, the sheep of his pasture.

If God says all these good things about us why do we allow the enemy to tell us lies? There isn't absolutely anything wrong with a woman enhancing her beauty through any method she chooses but according to Psalm 139:13-15 God sees no flaws with our appearances. We may not look like other people but we are not ugly because we do not. God has all sizes in his kingdom everyone can not be small or tall. It does not matter about your weight or height. I've struggled with insecurity for many years I was 120 lbs during these seasons. So, it does not matter your size. There were many women who felt good about themselves that weighted 200 lbs. SIZE DOESN'T MATTER!!! Yes, we should strive for healthy living but we need to be confident within ourselves. God has all kinds of shades. A lighter complexion woman is not prettier than a dark woman and vice-verse. We all are beautiful in God's eyes. I had to remind myself daily that I am fearfully and wonderfully made. I celebrated God's creation! I stopped using language that tore my self-esteem down. We often say things like, "Girl, I'm getting so fat", "Girl, I look so ugly in this dress", or "Girl, I'm not his type". These phrases seem extremely harmless. However, think how you feel when you say things like this. Instead, change your language from, "Girl, I look so ugly in this dress," to "Girl, this dress does nothing to embrace my beauty," or "Girl, I'm getting so fat" to "Girl, I'm going walking to enhance my beauty." We shouldn't downplay God's creation with negative words. We will always have an enemy to speak negatively over us. We do not want to become our own enemy.

God sees you Successful!

God wants all of his people to have success in every area of their lives. I stated earlier, we shouldn't fight each other to make a name for ourselves. God has a plan and he knows if we follow his guideline we will be successful. He wants to give us hope and a future. You may have experienced shame for years but God says he does no harm to his children. *Fear not; you will no longer live in shame. Do not be afraid; there is no more disgrace for you. You will no longer remember the shame of your youth and the sorrows of widowhood. Isaiah 54:4 NLT* The number one reason people fear following their visions and dreams is the feeling of not being smart enough. If God gives you a vision he will also give you the wisdom to bring that vision to past. I am not against education but God will give a high school drop out the wisdom to start and maintain a successful business. According to James 1:5, we only have to ask for wisdom. I know a local pastor that never went to school to become an architect but God gave him the wisdom to build a house. God will give the necessary resources to do the necessary plan however, it takes faith. God does not need us to become consumed with the "hows" that we forget about the "who". God is the "who" that will help us realize our goals. I believe we should do all we can to have the spirit of excellence. I have earned two degrees but some things I've learned concerning business was from God's word. Anyone pursuing a business should study the book of Proverbs. It gives you everyday principles and guidelines to become successful in marriage, relationships, and businesses.

There is only one you

You can discover a Christian's personality by the fruit they bear. The fruit of the spirit is the personality of people. People that are short tempered have no self-control. People that think holiness boldness is being mean really have no gentleness. God created a brilliant person when he created you. You are beautiful, successful, smart, and full of personality. You Rock!

Any person that can not see what God sees in you needs to be DISMISSED! At one point I had to dismiss everyone familiar out of my life to see myself the way God saw me. I was tired of believing what people had told me. People that knew about my past would constantly bring it up when I was trying to create a better future for myself. I had to remind myself daily that I was not going to be an enemy to myself. I was going to love myself and allow God to rebuild what people had torn down. People laughed at me because I posted a reading titled, "I am Special" in my bathroom mirror. I did that so every time I heard a negative comment about myself I would override it with the poem. I quoted the scripture many times to myself, *I will praise thee; for I am fearfully and wonderfully made: marvelous are thy works; and that my soul knoweth right well Psalm 139:14 KJV* I wasn't trying to become arrogant but rather healthy about the way I felt about myself, after all, I am God's creation. It is so important that we know who we are in Christ. People who know who they are in Christ are easier to get along with. There are so many people in the body of Christ that have identity crisis. They have a problem seeing the goodness of God at work in them because people will tear down what they do not understand. We are to be humble but we must have confidence in God. People have a misconception about self-confidence within the church and believe you are full of pride. I never said that people should feel they are greater than anyone else but to feel good from within. God does not want his people walking around with their heads down in the dirt. God can not get any glory like that. *Being confident of this very thing, that he which hath begun a good work in you will perform it until the day of Jesus Christ. Philippians 1:6 KJV* Insecurity was around in the bible days also. The children of Israel had problems with seeing themselves the way God saw them. Numbers 13:33 says, **"And there we saw the giants, the sons of Anak, which come of the giants: and we were in our own sight as grasshoppers, and so we were in their sight."**

Since, the children of Israel saw themselves as grasshoppers; their enemies viewed them as grasshoppers. The way you see yourself is exactly how others will see you. Perception has everything to do with your victory. *The children of Israel were negative and had the audacity to get upset with Moses, Aaron and God because they were not receiving the promises of God. (See Numbers 14)* Please do not make the mistake of blaming anyone for where you are now. The only two people that can control your life are God and you. You need God to direct you when pursuing your dreams but it take your positive thinking and initiative for it to come to pass. Sorry it was just a cliché to, "Just name it and claim it." Faith without works is dead. Many people believe that positive thinking is unnecessary. This is so far from the truth. I do not know about you but I hate being around negative environments. The negative mood sometimes causes me to feel negative about myself. Paul told us to keep our thoughts toward good things not on the negativity we are facing. ***Fix your thoughts on what is true and honorable and right. Think about things that are pure and lovely and admirable. Think about things that are excellent and worthy of praise. Philippians 4:8 NLT***

Why Do I Feel This Way?

Why do you feel the way you do about yourself? Is it your negative circumstances that makes you feel this way? Or, is it because people have made you view yourself this way? Before you go any further in this book, please be able to answer these questions so we can examine what you need to change. If you feel bad about yourself due to your circumstances you can shake yourself right now. Circumstances can change any day now but you can not allow your circumstances to make you feel bad about yourself. One phone call from a fortune 500 company can change your social status from an unemployed struggling single mother to the Vice President of Marketing. Do not allow your circumstances to label you. You may experience divorce but that does not mean you are going to be lonely the rest of your life. That's why people can not celebrate too early in the game when it seems the unpopular people are falling. *Rejoice not against me, O mine enemy: when I fall, I shall arise; when I sit in darkness, the LORD shall be a light unto me. Micah 7:8 KJV* Sometimes the way you feel about yourself has to do with your environment and the people you allow in your circle. If you are hanging around negative people that only criticize and make you feel bad about yourself, then your perception of self will most likely change. If one person has told us we were ugly as a child, we believe it instead of what God said. Children grow up feeling a certain way about themselves because they lived with parents who say negative things about them. Little Susie thought she could become a movie star until her mother says only pretty thin girls can be actresses. Little Susie now feels she is ugly and incapable of becoming an actress due to her weight. Her mother shaped that perception for her when she was 5 years old. Now, Little Susie struggles with low-self esteem. I remember asking a little girl what she wanted to be when she grew up. She answered with so much confidence I want to sing. I said well do not allow anyone to take that from you. If you want to sing then sing. I want to hear you sing every time I see you. I love inspiring children and young people because I will never forget in tenth grade we were sharing our aspirations in my Physical Science class, at that particular time I wanted to join the Navy after high school. I told my Physical Science teacher my aspirations and in front of the entire class she said, "Only Smart Girls Can Join the Navy." I was deeply upset with her and skipped that class every period due to the embarrassment. She did not cultivate my core beliefs about me. The truth was I was extremely intelligent especially in Science but I was dealing with harassment with boys in school which made me depressed. As a result, my grades dropped tremendously. Parents, teachers, and any leader have the power to shape children's awareness of themselves whether it is positive or negative. It is so important that we are careful with the words we speak because words do hurt. Words hurt more than physical pain sometimes. I can not remember every time I was spanked by my parents but I do remember those lectures. I would rather be spanked than to hear an hour lecture on how I disappointed them. Your child or student may be the next president. We have to see our children's future. That's why the world is so messed up today because people do not take time to help cultivate their children's dreams. Especially within the black community, our children try to show us their artwork and we tell them to leave us alone we are on the phone. Unknowing, that little boy has the potential of Pablo Picasso.

Be Aware!

Self-awareness is so important to pursuing your aspirations and dreams. If you have not defined yourself how do you know where you are going? Also, this will help you in each area of your life. I allowed people to mistreat me because I did not know who I was in Christ. So, if someone labeled me I would accept it because I hadn't defined myself. But, once God showed me who I was in him it really does not matter people's opinions of me. Their opinions of me can not define who I am. We spend valuable time explaining ourselves to other people than being who we really are.

While it is true that we are to humble ourselves, God wants his people to be confident in him. Throughout my life, I have been timid and shy. Whenever I walked in a room I felt that I was small and inadequate. I often complained how managers and people treated me but it wasn't their fault. I viewed myself this way and that's how they viewed me. I honestly began to seek God about teaching me who I was in Christ. I was tired of changing myself due to people's comments and opinions of me. Often people would make suggestions on how I should change, from my appearance to my behavior. But, that was how God designed me and I was uncomfortable when I started changing for people. It is always better to obey God than man. However, I wanted to be accepted by these groups of people only to find out they weren't designed for my life anyway. People who can not accept you for you are not meant to be a part of your circle. People that are for you will try to build you up and not tear you down. Seriously, who wants to hear what's wrong with them all the time? Is that constructive criticism? Mostly, if the criticism comes from people who do not care about you it is fault finding. We have to be careful of fault finding and judging. Also, if the criticism does not make you better then rule it out. Is that going to build up your character or make you feel worse about yourself? So, why do you continue to allow people to hurt you? God will use some people in your life to help you get to your destiny. Therefore, I'm not saying you should isolate from everyone. I am saying to consult God about the people you hang around. Everyone is not for you. This does not mean you should mistreat people or you backbite. You love them and move on!

Chapter 3

Discerning Good Soul Ties and Bad Soul Ties

Good Soul Tie

Do you know you are going somewhere in life? Then, watch your environment! Your environment can motivate you to do amazing things in the kingdom or frustrate the purpose of God for your life. There are two groups of people in our lives who can either be sent by God or sent by Satan himself. Relationships can create soul ties. Good soul ties are people that will enhance the positivity within your life. These are the people that will motivate you to stay on the straight and narrow path. They will only speak the truth in love and never rejoice when you are falling short of God's glory. People that know you are walking in error and will not warn you are not meant for you. People who are ordained by God want to see your relationship with the Father grow and mature. However, people who always make negative comments about you going to weekly bible studies, and praying and fasting are people who are sent by Satan. His objective is to separate us from God. An example of a good soul tie is David and Jonathan. The bible says Jonathan became one in spirit with David, and he loved him as himself. *After David had finished talking with Saul, Jonathan became one in spirit with David, and he loved him as himself. From that day Saul kept David with him and did not let him return home to his family. And Jonathan made a covenant with*

David because he loved him as himself. Jonathan took off the robe he was wearing and gave it to David, along with his tunic, and even his sword, his bow and his belt. I Samuel 18: 1-4 Their spirits were knitted together which meant they had spirits alike which were good spirits. Most people hang around people that are like them. I promise if a person has a nasty spirit they will hang out with people with nasty spirits or they will leave the friendship. This love was brotherly love which God commanded us to have, "love your neighbor as yourself". King David wrote a song for Saul and Jonathan after their death describing his love for Jonathan. Jonathan protected David from his own father, King Saul, who was jealous and had a quarrel with David. Jonathan and David's relationship was so deep Saul's animosity toward David did not strain their friendship. Many people believe that blood is thicker than water. However, when God is involved the relationship is closer than a blood relative. Within every relationship we will experience good and bad days. But, when the relationship is ordained by God all situations will work out for the good of the relationship. After a relationship has been tested, both parties should experience growth and reconciliation.

Bad Soul Tie

Bad soul ties are people that hinder you from God's purpose in your life. *My child, if sinners entice you, turn your back on them! They may say, "Come and join us. Let's hide and kill someone! Let's ambush the innocent! Let's swallow them alive as the grave swallows its victims. Though they are in the prime of life,*

66

they will go down into the pit of death. And the loot we'll get! We'll fill our houses with all kinds of things! Come on, throw in your lot with us; we'll split our loot with you." Don't go along with them, my child! Stay far away from their paths. They rush to commit crimes. They hurry to commit murder. Proverbs 1:10-16 NLT Most of the time you can tell if a person is a bad soul tie because they promote you to do sin. If you have to compromise your morals or mistreat people then these people will block your vision. Miserable people love to make other people miserable. People who have hatred towards other people need to be removed from your life immediately. As Christians, we must pray for people but you can pray for people at a distance. These people are really enemies to each other but will unite themselves for the purpose to destroy the innocent. They are out to kill people who are destined to do great things for God. They are sent by Satan and are extremely dangerous. It takes fasting and praying to destroy their schemes and plots. They will pretend to like you while secretly preying on you. *A bowl of soup with someone you love is better than steak with someone you hate. Proverbs 15: 17 NLT* According to this scripture, it does not matter if companions of friends eat a wealthy meal together, where strife and contention are there is no enjoyment. Unity brings the greatest pleasure in life. If your circle sows discord between you and other people you will always see the worst in other people. The wrong people will make your vision of yourself and others blurry. Whenever you are around them they make you feel bad about yourself. They always see your weakness and never compliment your strengths. They are extremely envious and

67

jealous behind closed doors. In public, you would believe that they wanted you to receive all God has for you until you share your dreams with them and watch their response. They will tell you all the problems why the dream can not come true. They weigh your soul down with gossip, lies, deceit, and discord. Soul ties do not necessarily have to be a love relationship. It could be a friendship, church members, co-worker, or any other relationship. ***Do not be yoked with unbelievers. For what do righteousness and wickedness have in common? Or what fellowship can light have with darkness? 2 Corinthians 6:14 NIV*** We often use that scripture for marital relationships but this is any relationship. You create soul ties by bonding with people out of your soul. You tell them intimate things about yourself and share quality time with them. Who you hang around really determines how you see yourself. There is a saying every bird of the same feather flocks with their own kind. This sounds cliché but it is the truth. Have you ever seen a crack head hang around an executive? No, not unless he is trying to get some alms. You have to hang around people that will celebrate you and the upcoming you. Even though we are not perfect and we all have flaws, it is nice to hear people congratulating your progress. It does not feel good when you've experienced failure and people around you constantly remind you of your past. Even though we may experience a season of hurt from separation you must get rid of all the bad soul ties.

Chapter 4

Seeing Your Suffering as Purpose

If we endure hardship, we will reign with him.

2 Timothy 2:12 NLT

Why Do Bad Things Happen to Good People?

Sometimes we feel if we are in a relationship with God we shouldn't experience seasons where we suffer and lose material things. Serving God has many benefits but sometimes we have to lose the first few quarters in order to win the entire game. Have you ever witnessed a basketball game where the losing team seemed defeated however one player successfully shoots a three pointer shot at the last minute and wins? It may seem like you are losing for years but one phone call changes your situation totally around. I can guarantee you that the suffering you are experiencing has a purpose. You may not see the purpose immediately but it will make sense after a while. God operates in seasons and there is a time for everything including suffering.

There is a time for everything,
a season for every activity under heaven.
A time to be born and a time to die.
A time to plant and a time to harvest.
A time to kill and a time to heal.
A time to tear down and a time to rebuild.
A time to cry and a time to laugh.
A time to grieve and a time to gather stones.
A time to embrace and a time to turn away.
A time to search and a time to lose.
A time to keep and a time to throw away.
A time to tear and a time to mend.
A time to be quiet and a time to speak up.

A time to love and a time to hate.
A time for war and a time for peace.
Ecclesiastes 3:1-1-8, NLT

This particular scripture is written on a cause and effect style meaning the "cause" makes something else happens. Your season of weeping prepares you for blessings that will cause you to laugh. You will appreciate laughing when life has tried to take everything away from you. People tearing you down through character assassination create a season for God to build you up through His grace. He would give you ten people to bless you for the ten people who persecuted you. You can not experience God's blessings if you are not willing to go through a season of suffering. The suffering I'm speaking of is suffering for well-doing. I know there are many Gospel Messages preaching sowing seeds of money will guarantee you a blessing from Heaven. I sincerely believe we should bless God's kingdom through giving but you will have to sow time, tears, warfare, and more things to receive the blessings of God. If you decide to throw twenty dollars on the altar do not expect to become a millionaire in seven days. You will have to work hard and save money and sow much more than 20 dollars. I've noticed that many people in my generation expect not to lose anything and wait as less as possible in order for them to call themselves blessed and highly favored. But, Jesus calls us blessed even in difficult times. ***Then Jesus turned to his disciples and said, "God blesses you who are poor, for the Kingdom of God is given to you. God blesses you who are hungry now, for you will be satisfied. God blesses you who weep now, for the time will come when you will laugh with joy. God blesses you who are hated and***

70

excluded and mocked and cursed because you are identified with me, the Son of Man. Luke 6:20-22, NLT It seemed as if Jesus had lost his sermon with the disciples. Jesus was calling people blessed that society would normally frown upon. This person was poor, hungry, sorrowful, hated, and an outcast but was called by Jesus blessed because there is always a blessing behind suffering. There is always a bigger picture. You lost a job? Then, enjoy the park, family, and close friends while you're waiting for the next door to open up. It is so important that people remain optimistic about their negative situations.

Keep Your Praise On

I attended a prayer meeting every Tuesday at a local ministry in Memphis, Tennessee. After every prayer session, we made a declaration "Keep Your Praise On!" During your time of suffering, it is not the time to sit on your bottom and close your mouth. It is time to praise God in your own way. If it takes screaming "Thank You Jesus" then you need to shout it from your belly. When bill collectors would call the house with harassing phone calls I would worship God for who he is. I declared with praise and not pity that God was Jehovah Jiriah my provider.   If you are going through you have a right to rejoice. I know we have heard many sermons promising the audience if we praise God through the storm a blessing is coming. It sounds cliché but it is a commandment from God that we rejoice in the day of trouble. Praising God helps us remain focus on our purpose. We were created to praise God regardless of our situations. *I will praise the LORD at all times. I will constantly speak his praises. Psalm 34:1, NLT* One Sunday, I was

71

praising God for his goodness and my clip-on pony-tail fell down in front of the entire church. I wanted to sit down because I was embarrassed. But, God told me to keep praising him. I praised God that Sunday until all my burdens were lifted. The enemy wanted me to sit down on my praise. But, God wanted me to praise him in spite of the embarrassment. I declared to God that I will become a consistent praiser. I would praise God regardless of how the enemy tried to embarrass me.

Even Jesus Suffered

Jesus is the best model for believers to follow during their season of suffering. People were willing to follow Christ as long as their journey with him was rewarding. However, when their relationship with Christ created opposition they disowned him. Simon Peter and another disciple were following Jesus during his miracle crusades, best teachings, and providing food for the hungry. But, people were not willing to follow him all the way. *Simon Peter followed along behind, as did another of the disciples. That other disciple was acquainted with the high priest, so he was allowed to enter the courtyard with Jesus. Peter stood outside the gate. Then the other disciple spoke to the woman watching at the gate, and she let Peter in. The woman asked Peter, "Aren't you one of Jesus' disciples?" "No," he said, "I am not." The guards and the household servants were standing around a charcoal fire they had made because it was cold. And Peter stood there with them, warming himself. Inside, the high priest began asking Jesus about his followers and what he had been teaching them. Jesus replied,*

"What I teach is widely known, because I have preached regularly in the synagogues and the Temple. I have been heard by people everywhere, and I teach nothing in private that I have not said in public. Why are you asking me this question? Ask those who heard me. They know what I said." One of the Temple guards standing there struck Jesus on the face. "Is that the way to answer the high priest?" "Is that the way to answer the high priest?" he demanded. Jesus replied, "If I said anything wrong, you must give evidence for it. Should you hit a man for telling the truth?" Then Annas bound Jesus and sent him to Caiaphas, the high priest. Meanwhile, as Simon Peter was standing by the fire, they asked him again, "Aren't you one of his disciples?" "I am not," he said. But one of the household servants of the high priest, a relative of the man whose ear Peter had cut off, asked, "Didn't I see you out there in the olive grove with Jesus?" Again Peter denied it. And immediately a rooster crowed. John 18: 15-27 NLT Peter denied Christ because he knew just being around Jesus would get himself into trouble. Sometimes just knowing Christ will create oppositions. Rejection and denial from people that are close to you are two different things. Rejected means to refuse to have, take, recognize but denied means to disown. Peter disowned Jesus even though they had so many experiences together. As matter of fact, Jesus had made Peter successful and productive where as at first he was a struggling fisherman. (Read Luke Chapter 5) It is so amazing how the people you have helped the most would be the ones that deny or disown what God is doing in your life. If Jesus had delivered Peter on so many different

occasions why would he not trust that Jesus would bring him out of this situation? If I walked with Jesus and saw him perform so many miracles in the past; I question if I would have had Jesus' back. However, like Peter we sometimes forget about our past victories to help with our present sufferings. Jesus was the Son of God and he did not deserve the treatment he went through. If you read the entire chapter of John 18 you will notice that after Jesus had finished praying that's when he started his suffering. He had been betrayed by Judas, Peter denied him three times, and he was physically abused. People did not just kill him with their mouths they physically hurt him. This physical abuse wasn't a minor bruise. They tortured Jesus. Although he was the Son of God, he wasn't in a divine body. His form was in human flesh so he felt every pain so he could relate to us. *For we have not a high priest which cannot be touched with the feeling of our infirmities; but was in all points tempted like as we are, yet without sin. Hebrews 4: 15 KJV* People rarely talk about Jesus weakness in Gethsemane but at one point Jesus was tempted to give up. *Then cometh Jesus with them unto a place called Gethsemane, and saith unto the disciples, Sit ye here, while I go and pray yonder. And he took with him Peter and the two sons of Zebedee, and began to be sorrowful and very heavy. Then saith he unto them, My soul is exceeding sorrowful, even unto death: tarry ye here, and watch with me. And he went a little farther, and fell on his face, and prayed, saying, O my Father, if it be possible, let this cup pass from me: nevertheless not as I will, but as thou wilt. Matthew 26:36-39 KJV* Jesus knew that he was about to go through a great deal of pain for God's sake. Jesus had the power to stop the torture but he did not because he had to fulfill his purpose which was dying on the cross for our sins. Our generation believes everything should be on a bed of ease. We are not taught that suffering for Christ's purpose is just as important. It builds our faith. The majority of messages preached today are about God rescuing us. There are many times in our lives where God wants us to grow and develop through those painful situations. While it hurts, we are learning the most valuable lessons. We are learning to have more compassion for other people. Our suffering is not just for ourselves but other people. I have heard many Christians confess that they do not have any problems well if that's the case I would reevaluate my relationship with Jesus. Throughout the bible, people were persecuted for Christ's sake. You will suffer if you belong to Christ. *Forasmuch then as Christ hath suffered for us in the flesh, arm yourselves likewise with the same mind: for he that hath suffered in the flesh hath ceased from sin; That he no longer should live the rest of his time in the flesh to the lusts of men, but to the will of God. I Peter 4:1-2 KJV* And he that taketh not his cross, and followeth after me, is not worthy of me. (Matthew 10:38) One day I was driving in my car on my way to class to become a licensed Evangelist for the Church of God in Christ. As I was driving the enemy spoke to my mind and asked, "How are you going to help other women overcome their past when you have one yourself? How are you going to lay hands on other people when you need healing yourself? How are you going to finance this vision when you are broke?" Sadly, I did not rebuke the enemy but I entertained him.

My strength was too weak to fight the enemy back so the tears fell down my face when I explained to God I wasn't the one to be an Evangelist. I had too many problems myself. I told him to get someone else that was perfect. Get someone that had the money to support the vision. God did not respond, so I kept driving. I drove until I found myself parked in the front of the building of my class. I felt this urge that I should go to class. I was so heavy that morning and was praying that the instructor would cancel class. However, class continued…..One of my classmates broke out in tears talking about how the enemy was coming on every hand in her home. Another classmate told her how she had overcame that situation. One classmate jumped up with excitement and told the class her story and how she had a testimony. Then, she explained that it was just cross duty. She said when I see people go forth in God I'm never impressed by their gift but impressed about the cost they had to pay for their anointing. She said, I want to know what it cost you to sing that song. What was the price you paid to deliver that message? She said if you think Satan is happy about you answering the call you can forget it. The closer you get to complete the assignment the more the enemy acts up. I felt it and rejoiced. I knew God had called me I was just serving cross duty. I had to deny myself and stop magnifying my problems. I knew God had called me and I was just going through so I could relate to people who needed Jesus. We are called to do diverse assignments but sometimes we allow the excuses to block our visions. You know God wants you to become an entrepreneur but your excuse for not starting the business is the startup cost. In that case, write the business plan and believe God for the money. He needs people to create jobs to stabilize the economy. Your calling does not have to be an Evangelist or Preacher. Do everything you can to bring that vision to past. It is God's vision so he will fund it. You have to deny the way you feel. I feel incompetent, fearful, and so on. But, deny your feelings! If you are not willing to deny your feelings for Christ's sake you are not worthy to be Christ's. Peter denied Jesus by being overly concerned about himself. He was trying to keep warm and wasn't thinking about Jesus. Although Peter had failed Jesus by denying him, God yet used Peter. God want us to be blessed but everything has its timing. I can relate to any person because of things I had to endure. I not only had to suffer but I had to endure the suffering. The word "endure" means to remain firm under suffering or misfortune without yielding. I had to learn to smile even though I felt like crying and to continue praising God like he had answered my prayers.

My Story of Suffering

There are several different reasons why people suffer. People shouldn't feel they suffer because they are evil it may be contrary. Job was an innocent man and God allowed him to suffer greatly. In 1993, during a New Years Revival, I dedicated my life to Christ under the ministry of Evangelist Barbara Jackson-Sago. I thought once I gave my life to Christ that life would be much more rewarding. However, I experienced a defining moment in my life that would change everything about me. I was in the tenth grade when God initially saved me from my sins. After that winter break, I was so excited to return to school and tell my friends about my spiritual experience with Jesus. However, being around Jesus created many enemies from my high school. Instead of being most popular, I became most hated. When I returned to school things had changed and I was getting ready to know God in a real personal way. During homeroom I walked in excited, I sat at my desk to prepare for a day of learning. There were ten guys in the back room giggling and whispering. I thought nothing of it because they were the class clowns. But, the giggling and whispering was about me. After class, one of the guys came up to me saying the most perverted things to me. I actually was shocked. Often during and after class, I was tormented by guys in my classroom. I remember one football player walked behind me saying awful things to me, he even pulled the back of my hair calling me a whore and other degrading names. I did not understand why I was experiencing these things since I gave my life to Christ. How could God allow this to happen to a teenager that recently gave their life to him? However, I was told that a rumor was out throughout the entire high school I allowed several members of my high school football team to run a train on me. This was a lie that was setup by Satan to destroy my name. During the remainder of my ninth and half of my tenth grade year, I was tormented through bullying. On the bathroom walls, my name was slandered with horrific lies. I was harassed on the bus, lunch, in class, everywhere I went everyday. My grades dropped tremendously and I did not participate in any extracurricular activities. I used to love to sing and I sang in the Concert Choir but I begun to skip that class. I had no friends and was too embarrassed to tell my parents what I was experiencing

I thought they wouldn't believe me. Things had gotten so out of hand that I began to skip school just for some peace. I wouldn't eat or sleep. I wore baggy clothes to avoid showing my femininity. I felt ugly and low about myself. The treatment went from harsh words to physical harm. Once in gym class, while I was doing pushups, four guys sexually assaulted me. One of the guys made me do push-ups and while I did them he did degrading things (some things are still too embarrassing to tell). The entire class did nothing but laughed. When I encountered one of my peers from high school I wanted to confront him. I was so full of rage and anger. A year ago, I ran into one of them at a local grocery store. I wanted to confront him so badly. He spoke to me; I wanted to say you know what you did to me. I had wonderful parents but I did not tell them because I wasn't comfortable talking to them about my problems. Teens should talk to someone about bullying, rape, and sexual assault whether it is a teacher, principal, or youth advisor at church. I didn't tell anyone because I was ashamed. I felt nasty, shame, and violated. I felt that they were more powerful than me. For years, they had my power! Until, I decided to use what was taken from me to help others. I can't be silent anymore! I can't get those years back. If I could I would have fought for justice. I had every right. I didn't know my rights. For years, I couldn't understand the anger I had towards men. Until, I realized that what happened when I was 15 would carry on in my twenties. It hindered me from healthy relationships. Sometimes teens feel that telling someone means they are weak. However, it is a serious problem for teens. It makes you feel weak and insecure of yourself and can lead to other serious problems. One night I went home and Satan deceived me to believing that the only way out was to take my life. I believed that if I took my life since I was saved I was going to heaven. I was looking for a way to escape. So, I took an entire bottle of my father's pain pills. Around two that morning, my body began to have a reaction to the medication. Everything in my room looked dark and blurry. That particular night for some reason my grandmother had spent the night at my house. She knew something was wrong and began to pray while my father and mother rushed me to the emergency room. While I was riding in the car, my grandmother was still praying that God would give me a second chance. The defining moment in this situation was when a nurse came and whispered in my ear that God was not ready for me to come home yet. God spared my life and I recovered from suicide. This story has a correlation to the way I felt about myself. If I really knew who I was in Christ I wouldn't allowed a lie or being sexually assaulted, but I did. This is relevant to the end of this book so remember this; once I was released from the hospital I changed schools. I was always afraid that the past would follow me to my new school. I was afraid to tell people my name. Due to my previous experience, I became very shy and insecure about myself. During the same time, my mother was ill. So, it was very difficult for me. But, God healed her body and my life got better and God healed me in layers. It always gets better! Instead of me facing the people who hurt me, I ran. But, I am facing up now and telling my story. God was trying to teach me then to face adversity as a strong soldier. ***Endure suffering along with me, as a good soldier of Christ Jesus. 2***

Timothy 2:3 NLT So many times we run from the lesson God is trying to teach us. To the parents, sit down and talk to your children. High school was extremely hard for me. I did not want to tell people. But, bullying and harassment are forms of torment and it does affect children and teenagers. To the young girl or boy who may be facing rape, sexual assault or bullying in your school you do not have to tolerate it. Stand up for yourself and do not be afraid to talk to someone. God is a prayer answering God but sometimes we need to pray and take actions. Do not make the mistake like me and run from opposition because you will be running the rest of your life. Your destiny is too great for you to forfeit it by being a coward and finding the easy way out. My testimony of humiliation and attempt to commit suicide has taught me that there is purpose in suffering. The purpose of God allowing suffering in your life is for the future glory he wants to fulfill through you. *Yet what we suffer now is nothing compared to the glory he will give us later. Romans 8:18 NLT* The suffering is not only for you but for those God has called you to minister to. How can you lead where you have not been? How do you know God is a healer? How do you know God is a deliverer? People want to hear your story of how God delivered you not what you've heard.

Suffering has a unique way of establishing a relationship with God. There are some things that God delivers you from that you will never forget. You'll always love him for what he has done for you and God will give you double for your trouble. *Isaiah 61:7 says for your shame ye shall have double; and for confusion they shall rejoice in their portion: therefore in their land they shall possess the double: everlasting joy shall be unto them.* Shame has a way of making you feel low about yourself. See, the things I have experienced helped me to have compassion for people from all walks of life. I can not look down on anyone because I too know how it feels to be ashamed of who you are.

Your suffering does not mean you have done anything wrong in the eyes of God it maybe the opposite. In the bible, there was a man named Job. The bible described him as being blameless and upright. God allowed Satan to test Job by taking his possessions, family, and health. Once again, the bible says Job was blameless meaning he did not deserve any of this. Please read the entire book of Job it truly is a powerful story for understanding suffering. In all that was done to Job, he did not curse God. He continually served God and counted him faithful. During tough times, you need to find God in worship. This will allow you to magnify God rather than your problems. In the end of Job's suffering, God blessed the latter end of Job more than the beginning. Let God bless the latter end of your life. I guarantee you that everything you've experienced God will makes sense of it one day. When I was facing adversity I would always tell my mother that one day this will all make sense. Now, it does. I love myself more and will not allow the insecurity of others to make me insecure.

Purging Process

At one point in my life I lost everything. I lost my apartment and my furniture. I felt like a complete failure I was a college graduate without a decent paying job and a place to call my own. I was BROKE. So, broke I didn't have a banking account. Although I was experiencing so much pain, God was yet giving me favor. I wouldn't tell anyone but sometimes I would walk into church and people would bless me with gas money. They had no idea that I drove to church by faith. I was driving a Honda, Accord 2007 I had to give it back to the dealership because I couldn't afford it. I had several health issues but I couldn't afford health insurance. My health really started to fail me. I'm not the victim. This is my true life story! Its funny God wouldn't allow me to pity myself. He taught me how to sustain. I love God and how he handles me. One day I wanted a new dress for a church service God told me to go to Goodwill. I laughed. I was used to major retail stores not Goodwill. I went to Goodwill and I found a brand new dress for five dollars. Then he had me research the original retailer so when people asked me where I got the dress I told them the website. There was the bright yellow dress that was designed just for me. God is AWESOME. I'm not ashamed about shopping at Goodwill but I couldn't tell people about my struggle God wanted the glory out of my life. That night I looked like a million dollars on a five dollar budget. I was going through tribulations. I wasn't sleeping well because I worried and stressed about my future. I knew to trust God but I didn't understand the process. That's why I'm telling my journey I want you to stop worrying. God will take care of you. As I stated in the previous chapter, I was also dealing with a lot of rejection in relationships. I felt that no one really understood me. I remember one Sunday I had just returned from Little Rock, Arkansas from ministry. I experienced a great deal of hurt through ministry. I was hurt because I was

83

experiencing so much pain from the outside when I came to church I wanted to feel loved, peace, and for people to pour into me. I take full responsibility that I needed to forgive and ask for forgiveness. I know I am not perfect and I am not trying to paint the picture I was. It was just that I needed to be restored not torn down at that point I felt I couldn't get any lower. I reached my breaking point after that I was tired of being strong for ministry, my family, and myself. I had an emotional shut down. I hadn't slept within two days from that Sunday. I was hurt because I really did not have anyone I could lean on. I was going to give up on ministry, give up on my dreams, and really give up on myself. That is the truth. And, I was tempted to actually severely hurt someone. Around 7 am that morning a local pastor (Pastor Michael Stevenson) called me. I hadn't told anyone about my mindset or the devastation I have received. He told me that the Holy Ghost dropped my name in his spirit and at 6 am his church was interceding on my behalf. I broke down crying explaining I believed what God had spoken over my life it was the process that was getting to me. He invited me to his church that Wednesday for bible study and prayed and spoke life into my situation. That's when I knew it was more to me than what people could see. In his prayer, he touched my eyes and prayed that I stopped believing in what I saw in the flesh. I begin to visualize in the spirit where I was going.

From that point, I had to decide to walk in forgiveness not just for others but for myself also. I have made mistakes in ministry but I was trying to change. But, then I realize I couldn't change myself I needed God's help. It is not by power, nor might, but by God's spirit. And, when you are trying to change it can hurt when people do not give you a chance to become better.

"Father, forgive them, for they do not know what they are doing."

First step to forgiveness we have to remember that we have hurt people also. But forgiveness is so important when other people have caused you to suffer. *If you forgive others, you will be forgiven. Luke 6:37, NLT* You MUST give forgiveness to get forgiveness. Think of a time when you needed God to forgive you for something you felt was unforgivable. Every time you choose to walk in unforgiveness try to remember that incident. We are not greater than God. When we choose not to forgive we make ourselves gods. Who are we to charge anyone for their wrong done towards us, its God that forgives sins? People you have not forgiven have power over you. There is no one deserving of that power! I could have chosen to walk in unforgiveness with the guys in my school, in ministry, and in relationships but that would make me bitter not affect them. When you choose not to forgive then you become part of what they have done to you. They continue to live while we hold grudges and limit ourselves. I had to forgive even though my offenders left my soul fragmented. If I decided to walk in forgiveness it was God's responsibility to make me whole. I have struggled with unforgiveness. It is not an easy process. You must ask God to help you in this area. Some issues only can be resolved by fasting and praying. You must ask God to pull unforgiveness from the root unless Satan plants a seed of bitterness. When people hurt us we have to admit that it does not feel good and we need to be healed. In ministry, I have often heard people say get over it like it is that easy. I have tried to get over what people have done to me but the offenses played in my mind over and over again like a broken record. One day God told me to pray for my enemies like I prayed for myself daily. I found myself praying for my offenders more than I prayed for myself. After I continued this process for a while, I felt God lifting the hurt and the burden of unforgiviness. Many Christians will pretend they have forgiven people out of obligations because they hear it preached across the pulpits. However, they have not truly forgiven because they still talk about the offenses with other believers. It's a mask! God wants us to forgive sincerely. He wants us to forgive like he's forgiven us for our debts. ***But if you do not forgive others their sins, your Father will not forgive your sins. Matthew 6:15, NIV*** Hurting people want their offenders to pay for the debt they feel is owed to them. This particular attitude means you are acting as a judge and God is the only judge. The guys, church folks, and people I was in relationship with weren't my problem. I was. But, God delivered me through prayer, fasting, and TIME. It takes time to heal. Don't rush the process. This will cause you to be frustrated.

Chapter 4 Affirmation

My Suffering is a part of My Purpose
I must go Through This Chapter in My Life
I Will Not Worry
I Will Not Stress
I Will Not Fret
Because My Suffering Is Creating God's Glory for My Life
I Will Survive No Matter How Hard It Get's
It is More to Me Than This

Chapter 5

Seeing Your Rejection as a Blessing

**For the LORD your God has arrived to live among you. He is a mighty savior. He will rejoice over you with great gladness. With his love, he will calm all your fears. He will exult over you by singing a happy song."
Zephaniah 3:17 NLT**

Why Not Me?

I do not care how great a person maybe everyone wants to feel accepted by people they are associated with. No one wants to feel the emotion of being rejected. It is very painful and uncomfortable. Sadly everyone in his or her life will experience rejection whether it is from a company, a broken relationship, or even in the church. Rejection makes you question yourself, "What's wrong with me?" "Did I do something wrong?" "Should I change who I am?" The answer is nothing is wrong with you, no, you did not do anything wrong, and you definitely shouldn't change. Everyone will experience rejection at least once in their lifetime. Experiencing rejection does not mean we are unloved, inadequate, or a failure. We sometimes make the mistake of allowing rejection to define the rest of our lives. For example, we allow the rejection from past broken relationships determine if we'll ever find love again. We allow the people who are not accepting of our gifts to determine if we are going to give up on our visions. However, rejection was design to make us grow stronger and unlock our greatest potential. It wasn't designed to make us feel like a loser!

<u>Surprise!</u>

Most of your rejection will come from people and places you think should embrace your visions and goals. That's why some rejection is more painful than others. It is more painful to experience rejection from people that are closest to you. You've been married for 20 years. You would think by now your husband would love you and see you for yourself. After all, you are the glue to the marriage you give 80% and he only gives 20%. He once was near death and your hands helped assist his recovery. After he is well, he leaves you for a younger woman. That kind of rejection is more painful than being dumped after the second date because you have not invested a lot of time, tears, pain, and happiness. The wife has invested 20 years of her hard earned life and probably has made several sacrifices. This particular sister would probably need more time to heal because she has been rejected after she should have been celebrated. Often the people you do the most for (the people who should be celebrating you) will be the ones who will not accept you for yourself. The man is not looking at the sacrifices his wife of 20 years had made instead he is going after a fantasy that will never be fulfilled. The world would be a better place if people would stop chasing an illusion from the Devil. If that husband would have taken the time to see what that woman really meant to him the marriage would have been in bliss after his recovery. It is very uncomfortable when you are giving and people can not see the gentleness of your heart.

What do you do when you are surrounded around people that can not see the God in you? Especially when God has called you into that place and you're not there by choice. That place can be a church, workplace, home, or your social networks. It is difficult to reach your God given potential when people try to tear you down before you have finished your assignment God has called you to do. I am a witness that God will see you through. Before I completed my Evangelist license, I was rejected by the ones I thought should have been celebrating this chapter in my life. I grew up in the church so I wanted to help other women receive salvation and deliverance. Sadly, people would tell me, "You are going to make a disaster," "You are too young", "Whose going to listen to you." I could have listened to the negativity of some of my peers but I was determined not to stop pursuing my calling. I knew that everything I had been through was birthing a ministry that was unique, relevant, and effective. God would always send me encouraging words to override the naysayers' comments. He will send you ten people that will accept you to replace the ten that rejects you. Throughout the bible, God always exemplified a person that experienced rejection. For example, there was a woman in the bible by the name of Leah. The bible described Leah in Genesis 29:17, as having weak eyes, but her sister Rachael was beautiful. Leah and Rachael were both married to Jacob but he loved Rachael more than Leah. Throughout their marriage, Leah had to go the extra mile to please Jacob but he was never satisfied with her. Does this sound familiar? I see this especially among women, we are always trying to get someone to love us. God is so faithful to us. Genesis 29:31

says when the Lord saw that Leah was not loved, he opened her womb, but Rachel was barren. God loves his daughters and he will always take care of us. While God favored Leah, she still was trying to win Jacob's love. She named her first son Reuben thinking Jacob was going to love her. Leah had three sons and believed that Jacob was going to love her. But, sadly he still loved Rachael more than her. Finally, Leah had a fourth son and named him Judah (which means praise). I believe Leah came to the conclusion that Jacob couldn't see her for who she really was. Therefore, he was incapable of loving her. Please stop wasting your energy on people who can not see you for you. I spent so many years explaining myself to people that I lost sight on the woman God called me to be. I assume that Jacob was looking at Leah's outer appearance and couldn't see that she was a woman devoted to God and loved him unconditionally. Do not get so distracted by the physical characteristics that you miss the spiritual characteristics. I would like to reiterate about Leah's fourth son Judah (Praise). I think this was a defining moment in Leah's life. She found God in the midst of her rejection. While Jacob wasn't in love with Leah, God loved Leah and blessed the fruit of her womb. In her time, being able to have children was a blessing. This let's readers know that God can use your rejection as a blessing.

My Story of Rejection

I can relate to Leah because I too know how it feels to lose someone you love. At the age twenty, I was in a relationship with a man I grew up in church with and I truly believed I had found my soul mate. We had plans to get married and have a family. I wanted for us to seek God together about the direction of our relationship. While I was seeking God about us, I dreamt that he had brought another woman to church. The next day my mother told me that he was seeing someone else and she was at church for bible study. When she told me that I felt a pain in the center of my chest it was almost if someone had hit me with a truck. Sadly, I stilled believed that there was some hope for us. As time passed, she came to church more often and I had to deal with knowing that another woman was with the man I loved. I remember one day going to the church restroom and crying myself to a headache. I wanted so badly to get over him that I did not allow God to heal me. I denied the fact that our relationship was over and pretended like I did not care. I went through a period of social isolation where I did not fellowship with any of the young people at our church because he was with them. Whenever you are experiencing problems do not allow Satan to isolate you from society especially not in the church. He's trying to isolate you to work on your mind. The enemy really began to work with my mind by telling me lies. Remember Satan is the father of lies. There were days when I would lock myself in the room. Again, I was humiliated and felt abandoned. The enemy knew I wasn't going to attempt suicide I learned my lesson from the previous experience. So, he tried to take my perception of life. In other words, I was in existence but I wasn't living the life God had designed for me. ***John 10:10 says the thief comes only to steal and kill and destroy; I have come that they may have life, and have it to the full.*** Since, I did not deal with the issues and I did not talk to anyone. I had a nervous breakdown and was admitted to a local behavioral hospital. I was so terrified I begged my parents not to leave. But, they had to do what was best for me. This was the scariest time of my life. It was the beginning of my womanhood I was 21 years old at the time. I hadn't heard of any young black woman at the time dealing with depression and anxiety. I questioned, "How a Christian woman could be going crazy?" I thought there was no way out. I was surrounded by bars and restrained from the outside world. When I first arrived I was admitted on the red zone floor which was designed for high risk patients. It was a nightmare! I wasn't eating, sleeping, and functioning on my own. I was totally in despair. This was the scariest moment in my life because I was away from my family and the church. I remembered looking outside a window with tears running down my face saying in my mind, "I'm going to always be this way". I would go two to three days without any sleep and I wasn't able to keep any food on my stomach. I would pace the hospital floors day and night. During visiting hours, my pastor at that time told me that the church was on a fast for my recovery. I began to see the results of the saints fasting and praying as my mind was being restored. The last day in the hospital God gave me the scripture ***Psalms 40:2-3 He brought me up also out of a horrible pit, out of the miry clay, and set my feet upon a rock, and established my goings. And he hath put a new song in my mouth, even praise unto our God: many shall see it, and fear, and shall trust in the Lord.*** While the church was on their knees praying, I walked in the church recovered from my nervous breakdown. I still praise God for this. After I was released from the hospital, God began to rebuild my life. I had to leave my church in order for me to get completely healed. When I first arrived to the church where God had me during that season the pastor would always say Jesus loves you. At that moment, I needed to hear that I was loved because I had experienced a lot of emotional hurt from my past. I knew that this church was for me and that I needed this church during this season. Not only did God restore my mind but he restored my dreams. I went back to school to earn my degree in Business Information Systems. God began to open many doors in my life and I was enjoying the journey. After receiving my degree, I was hired with the company I graduated from. I know this may sound cliché but sometimes God will allow circumstances to bring you into the greatest breakthrough in your life. I am a living testimony that every thing that happens in your life is for a purpose. When you were created, God knew the circumstances that you were going to face and he made a way of escape. But, you have to start seeing your rejection through the eyes of God or you will never get over the pain of rejection.

Now, this is not to destroy anyone's name. The guy I was dating at the age twenty was a very nice guy. We were not designed for each other according to God's purpose. There are no ill feelings towards him we both moved on. He has a wonderful family today and they are doing well. I'm only telling my story to encourage people to pursue who they really are. I'm not trying to tear anyone down.

When you experience true deliverance from an emotional crisis you must get rid of the residue also. Residue is remainder of something after removal of parts or a part. It took me falling on my knees asking God why I experienced the same pattern in my relationships. I was over the past relationship but noticed I had trust issues in every relationship I encountered. Even if it was a platonic relationship I always felt that men had a hidden agenda. It possibly could have stemmed from my high school experience and a failed relationship. However, I began to notice self-destructive behaviors. After I started working for a local department store, I met a handsome, tall, witty guy. He was so much fun and I was flattered when he asked me out. I never asked God prior to me dating him if he was my husband. First mistake, all life changing decisions should be consulted with God first. Remember he loves us and knows his plans for us. We both were members in the church and that meant we were for each other. However, at the time I had the residue of a past relationship and still suffered from my past. I really couldn't enjoy the relationship because I knew we were not for each other. I did not trust him and at the time he did not do anything to deserve distrust. After a year or so of dating, we were engaged to be married. Again, I did not seek God about him being my husband I was excited about getting married. But, I wasn't ready for marriage. I did not love myself at the time. Shortly, I called off the engagement. He was great also. I am so grateful to have experienced great guys but at the time I didn't understand that I needed a deeper healing. You will be wise to be by yourself and allow God to prepare you for his purpose. Instead, we hide behind relationships not designed by God to avoid dealing with the pain. And, at the time I needed some work done on me. I wanted deliverance and when you are desperate for deliverance the other parties' mistakes does not matter. You cannot control anyone but yourself. So focus on your strengths and weakness before you try to fix someone else's flaws. I know we do not like to be by ourselves especially women but sometimes it is required. After I called my engagement off, I took a hard look at myself. I asked God to help me discover love for self and heal the brokenness of my soul. See, if you do not have love for yourself it is impossible to accept love from someone else. Therefore, I believe both men truly loved me but I had issues. If you really want to see the greatness in you unlock you must take a look at yourself and see your weaknesses. Even after being in two serious relationships, I still was seeking love from men. If a man gave me any type of attention I was ready to plan the wedding the next day. This caused me to be hurt every time. I had to ask God where this behavior was stemming from. You do know that all behaviors derive from some type of source? So, I had to have space to search my inner man. This was not an easy process. It actually was the most difficult season of my life. I was extremely lonely. But, I heard Pastor Michael Stevenson say when we are trying to be delivered we sometimes experience withdrawals. Therefore, many times we have to be weaned off some things and people. It is going to be a process which requires prayer and fasting. ***Howbeit this kind goeth*** *not out but by prayer and fasting. Matthew 17:21* It took me being honest with myself and allowing God to purify me. I went through many different changes to get to where I needed to be.

During my process, I still was trying to fix my situation by looking for love in all the wrong places with the wrong motives. Every time it ended in disappointment. Instead of allowing God to finish his work in me, I covered it up with fake smiles, buying new clothes, dating someone different all the time. It took me looking closer at myself through the word of God for me to find the answer. I looked at myself I did not like what I saw in myself. I saw myself chasing things and people rather than chasing God. He promised that he would give me the things if I would seek him first. Matthew 6:33 I saw myself being what people wanted me to be. I even saw myself as this insecure little girl. A little girl that was lost in a world full of hurt, disappointments, and pain. A little girl that seemed stuck at age 15. And, I was tired. I grew up in church and I know that Jesus did not die and rise again for me to settle in life. I wanted the life that Jesus promised. *The thief comes only to steal and kill and destroy; I have come that they may have life, and have it to the full. John 10:10 NIV* I wanted to live!

I prayed that God wouldn't allow me to date anyone unless they were ordained by God. And, He kept his end of the covenant. Whenever I met anyone that wasn't designed for me God did not let it happen. I thought God was trying to make me into a junior St. Paul. *I say therefore to the unmarried and widows, It is good for them if they abide even as I. I Corinthians 7:8 KJV* I remember when I was stood up for a date. I couldn't understand and just begin to wonder if something was wrong with me. God kept reminding me I asked for the right mate. I wanted this time for Him to work on me. Also, I had to realize that some rejection was for my protection. We have to learn to accept what God allows. Acceptance to God's will show spiritual growth. We do not have to allow rejection to make us become bitter with the other party. If someone has rejected you it simply means you two weren't designed to complete the journey together. Why do we have to destroy each other's names due to a failed relationship? This can be in ministry also especially among leaders. We have to learn to let people go when they are ready to leave. Regardless, if they stay or not mentally it is over. This is why people experience hurt. You should never allow anyone to tolerate your existence rather than celebrate you. Most people tolerate people they are afraid to let go.

Learn to redefine yourself according to the Bible. The word of God described the essence of my character. I wasn't a doormat, playmate, or sideline girl. God created me to be a wife. I knew God made me a Proverbs 31 woman and I refuse to be anything less. I wasn't going to allow anyone else to treat me less than royalty because their eyes couldn't see my talents, anointing, and purpose.

Letting go of Rejection

Sometimes we are adapted to rejection we doubt acceptance. People have rejected us and it clouds our judgment to the people who accept us. We believe the people who love us have a hidden agenda. We box ourselves in to avoid future wounds. Fear will paralyze us from reaching our fullest potential. It was time to move pass my history and embrace my destiny. I was so serious about this process. I decided anything or anyone that was not adding to my life, I had to let it go. And, celebrate the new people in my life. That included dead end jobs, dead end relationships, and things I couldn't afford. And, learn to embrace my new season. This process was very difficult for me. There were times when I would be alone. Times when I felt no one understood me and times were I struggled financially. But, I knew I had to go through this process to help someone else. I was giving up everything to follow my purpose. Before I gave up anything, I consulted God first. You have to acknowledge him in everything you do. I knew it was time to let go of a company that constantly rejected my gifts and talents. There were so many days when I would cry because I had to go to a job I knew that limited my talents and abilities. I worked for a supervisor that wouldn't allow people to express their ideas and you had no voice. I went to work and gave it my all however there came a point when I would sit at the desk and felt empty. I begin to seek God about that job. I typed a two weeks notice to my supervisor but I wouldn't submit it until I received a clear answer from God. Well, God revealed his answer in an unexpectedly way. God was taking me on a journey that required me to trust him completely. I started a mobile jewelry company, further my education, and started writing my book.

Although I experienced rejection from my former employer, God was turning it around for a blessing. I saw the hand and power of God on so many instances in my life. I learned through my rejection seasons to embrace God's acceptance of me. God sent people into my life who helped me. I never asked anyone for money but he would lay it upon people's heart to give to me monetarily or buy products. I worked at local retail store making $8.25 but I was introduced to the retail industry. I learned the essence of the Merchandising Department and met some incredible people. God later opened the door for me to start at a better company which I currently work in the Corporate Office. I enjoy what I do. I really wish people would share their REAL testimonies you never know who you are helping. If I never became unfilled with my former job I wouldn't pursue "BETTER"!If I never worked as a college graduate making $8.25 I wouldn't have experience in Retail Merchandising. If I didn't have experience in Retail Merchandising I wouldn't be working in my current career. It's all working for your good be patient with the process. Please do not work at a job your entire life and hate it. Life is too short and you're investing too much time. 2080/plus hours a year doing something you don't enjoy is a waste of time. If you add up the time you would have invested approximately 72,800/plus hours within 35 years. Find what you created to do, you will be much happier.

We have to let go of rejection if we want to see the blessing out of it. What if I decided to allow the people who rejected me to quit my journey? God was trying to surround me around people that would embrace me and help me. We have to learn to ignore rejection and celebrate those people that mean us well.

In order to let rejection go, we have to know the symptoms of rejection. If you're experiencing any of the symptoms below you may have been rejected in your life.

Symptoms of Rejection

low self-image	feel insecure	withdrawn
personality		
condemn myself	hate myself	try to please others
feel worthless	believe I am a failure	agony within
feel inferior	question my identity	develop a facade
starvation for love	promiscuous	insecurity
inferiority	not worthy	fear of rejection
hate myself	self rejection	feel abandoned
accuse myself	can not accept love	failed relationships
can not give love	internal hurt/pain	can not love spouse
do not know who I am	earn acceptance by	depressed

Chapter 6

Seeing Failure as Success

Rejoice not against me, O mine enemy: when I fall, I shall arise; when I sit in darkness, the LORD shall be a light unto me. Micah 7:8 KJV

I've fallen and I can not get up

It does not matter how hard you have fallen in life just get up. It is easy to fall but extremely hard to get up that was my problem after all my rough life experiences. The rejection from my past experiences made it hard for me to get up. I did not want to hear no anymore so for a while I gave up. I gave up on business, ministry, relationships, and any other vision I had for my life. It seemed to be dimed for a while. However, in my innermost being (God) kept pushing me to get better. I had to keep quoting to myself it is more to me than where I am now. You've heard the saying, "Misery Loves Company". Everyone around me seemed successful on facebook, magazines, or let them tell it. However, I had to realize things are not what they appear. Everyone that is smiling on the outside is not happy. That's why we can not compare ourselves with other people or try to keep our social status with theirs. Most people that seem like they have it all together are really struggling behind close doors. Most people that rejoice in seeing other people down are already defeated. God told me I want you to give everything you have at this last push. Sometimes we do not give it our best shot. He did not want me to carry the visions in my head it was time for actions. I went from writing 1,000 words for my book daily to 10,000 words daily. I pushed. If I was told by someone that I couldn't own my own business I did more research. If I was told I interrupted service by praising God I danced the more. I prayed, fasted, read more about my vision for my life. I drained the negativity with positive beliefs. I was 30 years old now it was time to stop crying and help someone else. This was the main idea for me writing about my life stories. It wasn't so I could become New York's best seller I wanted to help people. I couldn't give up. If I chose to give up I would not only be giving up on myself but God, my reading audience, and young girls like me that struggle with insecurity. You can not give up because remember your Creator gave you the gift. If someone was to purchase you a Benz without any monthly payments, no insurance dues, and give you all the gas and maintenance money I'm sure you would gladly accept that gift. You wouldn't leave the Benz in the garage but show it off to the world. It is the same way with God, he gave us these gifts it does not matter if people can see them or not. It does not take the fact away that we are gifted. Paul told Timothy *"Do not neglect your gift, which was given to you through prophecy. 1 Timothy 4:14NIV.* Neglect means to pay no attention or little attention to. You must develop your gift. Some people think because you desire to display your gift or use your gift people are trying to be seen. Biblically, we are supposed to use our gifts for God's glory it's not about outshining another individual.

Regardless of my obstacles, I always knew that I was destined for greatness in God's kingdom. It had been spoken over my life by people and God had revealed it to me during my prayer time. While I knew I was going to be great for God's glory, I had to fight through labels and opposition. Everything I prayed for was going contrary to what God had said. I recall the parable that Jesus gave his disciples about the seed and sower. *Now the parable is this: The seed is the word of God. The ones along the path are those who have heard; then the devil comes and takes away the word from their hearts, so that they may not believe and be saved. And the ones on the rock are those who, when they hear the word, receive it with joy. But these have no root; they believe for a while, and in time of testing fall away. And as for what fell among the thorns, they are those who hear, but as they go on their way they are choked by the cares and riches and pleasures of life, and their fruit does not mature. As for that in the good soil, they are those who, hearing the word, hold it fast in an honest and good heart, and bear fruit with patience. Luke 8:11-15* If the enemy can get us not to believe in the word of God or make us forget it then we will not be productive. You can not look at your situation when God has spoken success over your life.

Many people completed college partying and enjoying their youth. My college years were a struggle. After I graduated with my associate's degree, I immediately began to pursue my bachelor's degree at a local college. I thought I was on the road for success but experienced a major roadblock. I was having a difficult time in my Biology class so I sought help from my professor. At first, he was very helpful and allowed me to work on an environmental program at the college. During the finals, I became very ill and asked if I could take my finals at a later date. He agreed and scheduled a retake exam during his office hours. I took the exam but failed the exam. He knew that I had been struggling the entire semester so he told me I wouldn't fail the class. I was excited until he closed the door and sat on the sofa I was sitting on which made me very uncomfortable. He said he would pass me on one condition if I went out with him. I told him no and was very firm with my response. Behind closed doors, I was sexual harassed by a professor that I had a lot of confidence in. Once again, I blamed myself for what was done to me. I asked God how I could constantly face circumstances like this. I did not dress inappropriately as matter of fact I was conscious about misrepresenting myself. I am quiet so I wasn't in his face all the time. So, what was the problem? I always wanted men to like me for my character or intellect not my body. I reported him and I eventually left that school the next semester due to the way my case was handled. I was deeply affected by this situation. I went through social isolation where I did not hang out with my family and friends. I think I became bitter with men. Sometimes God will close one door so he can open a better door. I did not allow my experience to hinder my dream of obtaining a bachelor's degree. I went to several other schools and today I have my Bachelor's degree in Business Administration with a concentration in management. If I did not experience the trouble I had to go through I would not have been able to write this book.

Failure does not mean that you failed sometimes failure is a setup for a much greater success in the future. I'm glad about my experiences because I know God was setting me up for the biggest breakthrough in my life. Today, I'm glad that God closed the door for marriage because he kept me from marrying the wrong person. It does not mean that something was wrong with that particular person it only means that we were not meant for each other. So many times in my career I did not get the promotion and I'm happy about that too. I did not want to retire from that particular company.

Stepping into the Water

Failure is inevitable! It will happen if you plan to become successful. You may have to try a business plan seven times before you see the success of a business. In those moments, it can be difficult to get up. There will be times when we have fallen down and need assistance with getting up. *For though the righteous fall seven times, they rise again. Proverbs 24:16 NIV* Often we quote that scripture to mean sin only. But, it also can mean fall in business, ministry, marriage, or any other activity. During this time, there isn't anything wrong with asking for assistance as long as it does not become a permanent situation. I needed government assistance and did not allow anyone to make me ashamed. The moments I needed assistance I dressed as if I was yet working in Corporate America. I did not allow the system to dictate who I was. When I was working I was very professional and continued to be that way. I just experienced a temporary setback. Whenever Jesus came he not only saved people souls but he blessed their economic situation. There was a lame beggar in the bible that needed to be healed and delivered from poverty. The biggest lie from the enemy is that God wants his children to live in sickness and poverty. But, Jesus changed this man's life and he went to tell everyone. *One day Peter and John were going up to the temple at the time of prayer at three in the afternoon. Now a man crippled from birth was being carried to the temple gate called Beautiful, where he was put every day to beg from those going into the temple courts. When he saw Peter and John about to enter, he asked them for money. Peter looked straight at him, as did John. Then Peter said, "Look at us!" So the man gave them his attention, expecting to get something from them. Then Peter said, "Silver or gold I do not have, but what I have I give you. In the name of Jesus Christ of Nazareth, walk." Taking him by the right hand, he helped him up, and instantly the man's feet and ankles became strong. He jumped to his feet and began to walk. Then he went with them into the temple courts, walking and jumping, and praising God. When all the people saw him walking and praising God, they recognized him as the same man who used to sit begging at the temple gate called Beautiful, and they were filled with wonder and amazement at what had happened to him. Acts 3:1- 10 NIV Notice* that this man's situation put him at the gate of Beautiful, he did not ask to be there but he was lame from his mother's womb. Most people in our society did not ask to be in their current situations. Most of the competent people are unemployed. They did not ask to be without work causing them to need government assistance. Most people on disability would love to be healed and work for a living. I know there are many people who can do better and are lazy. We still need to pray for their minds. Sometimes people become familiar with what they have seen in their families and communities. However, that's not all cases. For one, I know I was a hard worker. I did everything that was told to live the American Dream. I went to college and worked a part-time job. But, I too had to stand in the unemployment line one day. Sometimes people judge people because they have not lived in another person's shoes. People had to carry this lame man around town and his occupation was to beg alms. He had become familiar with receiving money from other people. The bible stated that he expected to get something from them. Peter does not have any money to give but he gives this lame man something far more valuable than money. He gives him Jesus which changes this man's life. The transformation I want people to have is a life changing experience. If you would notice whenever a person had an encounter with Jesus their life was never the same. That's why I tell people going to church alone will not transform your life without experiencing Jesus Christ. Jesus not only heals this man's cripple state but he gives him power to get wealth himself. He no longer has to beg for alms due to a disability. He is standing on his own two feet and can work for his living expenses. God wants you to stand on your own two feet. You are no longer lame by your past, poverty, or anything else standing in your way of destiny. Jesus wants to give people the power to become an overall better person. Once we give our lives to Jesus people will recognize the transformation. The lame man goes into the temple courts telling what God has done. When people noticed this lame man who sat at the gate called Beautiful walking and jumping, and praising God they were amazed at what had happened. God is going to do something radical through your life that will not only bless you but also bless the nations.

Chapter 7

Seeing your Future, After a Horrible Past

As far as the east is from the west, so far has he removed our transgressions from us. Psalm 103:12 NIV

Many people can not embrace their best life now or future because of their past. I know that the past will make you feel unloved but it will also make you feel unworthy. I stated earlier that I couldn't see myself married, in a thriving career, or my business restored because I failed in the past. But after experiencing a horrible past, we have to believe life gets better with time and effort. People will move quicker into their destinies if they could let go of the past. However, sometimes our past holds us tight while our future seems so distant from us. Answer, one important question for me. What do you want? The reason for me asking this question is because many times the enemy will make us believe our past was greater. We have become adapted to failed relationships, failed plans, and failed ministries. It wasn't working back then, "Get Over It!" This is for the singles! I often prayed for God to send me a husband who loved God. As a single woman, I had the list. 1. Must love God. 2. Must be faithful to church. 3. Physically Attractive. So on and so on… I had standards to the ideal guy I wanted God to bless me with. However, when I dated someone I would overlook 1 and 2 on my list because I was tired of being lonely. I felt if I was physically attracted to him I could change 1 and 2 on my list. It always ended in disappointment and hurt.

I did not understand that attending church did not necessarily mean a guy loved God. I experienced one failed relationship after another. However, one failed relationship from my past almost cost me my life. When we first started dating we prayed together over the phone, went to church functions together, and I had introduced him to my family. I thought he was the real thing for my life. We dated for approximately seven months consistently. He normally called before he went to work daily. One night he texted me one day before my 29th birthday and said he wasn't ready for a relationship. I did not receive any warning about him breaking up with me. I remember that text literally knocking me on my knees. I felt that feeling again like I was hit by an 18 wheeler truck. After that I spent months, trying to figure out what was wrong with me. I went through several events during my life trying to get free. I would allow him to come in and out of my life. He even confessed to dating another woman. But, when I realized who I was in Christ I had to stop allowing myself to be a doormat to the enemy. I prayed everyday that God would get him out my life. Not that he was a bad person I just did not like the person I was becoming while I was dating him. With much fasting and prayer God delivered me from that failed relationship. After I became free, the past wouldn't let me go. One New Years, he called and asked if he could see me. You know how the enemy works. I agreed to see him. One day I was sitting at my desk and God told me I couldn't go. God began to minister to me and ask me, "Is this what you want". He wasn't the ideal

0 husband for my life. The few good memories were overshadowing the horrible memories I experienced. I allowed myself to go through a lot with a man that wasn't my husband. I refused to return to my past. I worked hard with God to get delivered. In Louise Hay's book, *You Can Heal Your Life* she talks about letting the past go. She stated that, *"we need to release the past, let it wash away. Take back your own power. Stop dwelling on what you do not want. Use your mind to create what you do want."* I did not want him but I was willing to settle. It wasn't anything wrong with him but he did not fit God's plan for my life. I did not fit his plan for his life as well. God told me to cancel the date and wait on him. There is no reason to waste time. I held on to the memories that brought me happiness rather than the times I experienced hurt. I wasn't willing to let the past go. But, when I decided to let the past go, good memories and bad memories vanished. When we experience salvation it does not mean we will forget all our memories immediately. You know sometimes the enemy will bring up flashbacks. But, we have to rebuke those flashbacks and move forward to our purpose. Ending always mean that a beginning is coming. We have to become mature and know that relationships sometimes end. That can be friendships, romantic, in ministry, or as co-workers. It does not mean that we are the problem or others are. The past does not determine our futures unless we decide to hold on to it. Yet, we hold on to dead-end relationships, dead-end jobs, and dead-end dreams because we are not willing to let the past go.

We have to embrace the future God is trying to take us. What if someone invited you to an all expense paid exotic vacation for a long period of time where you couldn't pack any bags. Would you go? I guarantee most people will be on that flight within the next hour after receiving the phone call. That's how God's plan works for a new thing. *Behold, the former things are come to pass, and new things do I declare: before they spring forth I tell you of the. Isaiah 42:9 KJV* He wants to take us to another place but our past hurts and disappointment can not go. If we packed our past with us to a new place we will never experience the abundant life. Or, we would become so bitter from our old place we make other people's lives difficult. Past baggage burdens you down with fear, shame, guilt, hurt and disappointment which carries over to the new place. We need to learn to prepare for our new place while we are waiting to be delivered. For instance, you know your season is up with the company you've worked for ten years. You're not working with passion or zeal anymore you're just going through the motion of the daily routine. You've experienced much confrontation with the boss, customers, and co-workers. It is so important for you to restore those relationships before considering taking another job. First of all, God is our source but we need other people to get to the next level. It would be difficult to receive a good reference from people because we were out of our Godly character. Also, if you're the problem you need to work on self. Ask yourself if I'm not getting along with co-workers because I'm rude or self-fish. If it is you then you need to become a better "You" if it is them then you need to be healed from your previous employer. The bible says owe no man anything we believe that mean monetarily but we sometimes can owe people apologies. *Owe no man any thing, but to love one another: for he that loveth another hath fulfilled the law. Romans 13:8 KJV*

Chapter 8

Seeing God's Directions

In your unfailing love you will lead the people you have redeemed. In your strength you will guide them to your holy dwelling.
Exodus 15:13 NIV

God's Guiding Light

Before you begin to start your journey to a new "you", ask God questions. Often I felt like I couldn't ask God anything about where I was or going because I thought asking God questions was being rebellious. We are taught to never ask God why in the church. Asking God why meant questioning his wisdom or nature. That wasn't true!!! The bible says in Proverbs 3:6 in all thy ways acknowledge him, and he shall direct thy paths. God wants you to acknowledge him in all your decisions. Remember he is the Lord of your life which means he manages all affairs. For so many years, I have done things the way I wanted things to be done. I missed so many opportunities because I did not ask God questions which caused a mess in my life. When I started to ask God questions about my life then I noticed progress. There wasn't anything in my life that I did not pray about first. I asked God about my career, my future husband, my future, etc. Now, God gave me the gift of freewill so I did not ask him what to wear to work or things of that nature. I do not want anyone reading this book to take that out of context. I'm referring to things that have consequences by the choices we make. We would avoid marrying the wrong person if we acknowledged God about who we dated. We believe because they are physically attracted and successful God is in it. The Devil has tricks! Later you will find out that person is the reason your ship is sinking. Their credit is bad, attitude is bad, and temper is bad. In the beginning, people would put on a front just to get access. As days, months, years go by their true colors will be revealed. Prayer warriors become Prey Warriors. God knows all things! He knows people's hearts and motives. You could have avoided that trial by leaning not to your own understanding. But, sometimes we are in a hurry to get what we think we want. Many times God warns us about the people we date but we ignore that still small voice over a filet mignon. People are revealing themselves to us all the time but all we see is tall, dark, and handsome. Some people are counterfeits sent by Satan to distract God's purpose in your life.

Often people choose career paths because growing up they were expected to follow this path. Remember, Little Susie she wanted to be an actress but her mother thought she wasn't pretty enough. Her mother thought she should have pursued being a teacher. Little Susie is grown and miserable now because God created her to be a Christian Actress but she was distracted by her mother's own agenda. Most ideas that come to us are not from ourselves. God put those ideas so he can get the glory. We allow what people say about us matter more than what God says. If God gives you an idea he will support it financially and guide you through each step.

Once, I asked God about the people I allowed in my life the value of my life change. Before, I was doing things on my own and valued the wrong people. People who really supported me and had my best interest in mind I thought was against me and the people who I valued were against me. I was blinded by Satan. Since, I changed my circle of friends many people believe that I am conceited which is not true. The bible says iron sharpens irons which mean you can not expect to be an eagle hanging around birds. You hang around messy people, and then you will become messy. He said/she said is not valid information. It is very frustrating to hear grown people talk about what they heard. Now, if we are Christians we shouldn't entertain gossip. If someone tells you that somebody else said something negative about you then do not you think the other party put their two cents in also? There are different reasons people come into your life. Some people are added to your life only for a season. Sometimes you can give seasonal people too much information, time, and energy.

Chapter 9

Seeing Insecurity as a Danger

"A competent and self-confident person is incapable of jealousy in anything. Jealousy is invariably a symptom of neurotic insecurity."
- Robert A. Heinlein

Dealing with the insecurity of others

Have you ever arrived in a room filled with people and their response to your presence is an up and down stare? You immediately ask yourself is there something wrong with my appearance or did I say anything wrong. People will automatically judge you within five minutes and form a false opinion of you. But, my growth in life has helped me to understand that insecure people are often threatened by other people. The chapters you have previously read are to help you see yourself. First, we are to examine ourselves before we examine others. Now, I want to focus on external situations that shape our core beliefs about ourselves. This chapter focuses on insecurity of other people. Insecurity is when a person is not confident or sure of themselves. Many people who are not sure of themselves will always try to make you feel unsure about yourself. Being comfortable within your own skin will cause people to hate you. People will often attempt to change what they do not understand. You do not have to explain yourself to others. I made this mistake for many years. Until I decided that defending myself was for the birds and I am an Eagle. The body of Christ must understand our goal is the same which is to bring glory to God but we all are different. We all have different styles of worship, fashion, and views. Insecurity comes when we compare ourselves with others in the body of Christ. As I stated previously, I know many women of God that I admire in ministry. However, I am extremely careful about mimicking others. I love doing what God has called me to do because I enjoy being who he has made me to be. If you really want to unlock your potential you cannot try to mimic other people. I see this throughout the body of Christ today. Many people do not realize that imitating someone else robs themselves and the person they are imitating. It is also a sin according to ***Galatians 5:19-21 Now the works of the flesh are manifest, which are these; Adultery, fornication, uncleanness, lasciviousness, Idolatry, witchcraft, hatred, variance, <u>emulations</u>, wrath, strife, sedition, heresies, Envying, murders, drunkenness, revellings, and such like: of the which I tell you before, as I have also told you in time past, that they which do such things shall not inherit the kingdom of God.*** Emulation means to strive to equal or excel, especially through imitation. Many people in the body of Christ have competition and God isn't being glorified. We are competing for positions, favoritism, and a social status and have left what is most important which is winning souls. I have reached the point in ministry where I would let the people have the church work, lead me to somebody on the street that needs to hear about Jesus. Ministry is more than being within the four walls of the church to me. I want to minister to people who are hungry for Jesus. I have no time to waste on competing with insecure people in the body of Christ for titles and positions. When we realize what lane we are traveling in and continue in that particular area

117

then greatness will arrive in us for God's glory. We have accidents when we begin to travel in other people's lanes. If your gift is music then why are you serving on the Usher Board? Your personality is not made to serve on the Usher Board. You have a low tolerance for people and never smile. I guarantee if that person is serving on the Usher Board and was gifted in music they will be miserable and misery loves company. You are serving in your area God has gifted you in and they will be upset just because you know who you are in Christ. The body does not function well if members are out of place.

<u>People are not Your Enemy</u>

There are key points to survive persecution because it will surely come if you are Christ's. First, you need to recognize that people are not your enemy but Satan is. *For we wrestle not against flesh and blood, but against principalities, against powers, against the rulers of the darkness of this world, against spiritual wickedness in high places. Ephesians 6:12 KJV* When you are operating in your calling to the glory of God you will have spiritual enemies to hinder our Christian work. These enemies are not seen with the natural eyes therefore many times we mistake people as our enemy.

When people give Satan place he will use them to fight against you. You may not understand why that lady at the workplace gives you problems after all you were at peace with her. She may be dealing with a truckload of insecurities and picks on you because she thinks you have it together. So, take it as a compliment and stop trying to seek revenge and pray for her. In chapter one, we discussed God's love for us. Now, that we have defined God's love we should practice walking therein, even if that person has hurt us multiple times. *Jesus answered, "I tell you, not seven times, but seventy-seven times. Matthew 18:22 NIV* Now, it would be impossible to keep record of offences after the seventh time so imagine trying to keep record seventy-seven times. In other words, forgive how many times you need to. Jesus taught on love throughout his ministry because he knew the world would see God through our love. I have outlined several scriptures on practicing love on other people.

Before my stage of maturity, I fought with my mouth which made my situation worse. *But no man can tame the tongue. It is a restless evil, full of deadly poison. James 3:8 NIV* I did not understand the importance of holding my peace and allowing God to fight my battles. Some words can wound people for a long period of time. Also, we can destroy friendships, opportunities, and our perception of ourselves by the words we speak. *Death and life are in the power of the tongue; and they that love it shall eat the fruit thereof. Proverbs 18:21 KJV*

The latter end of *Ephesians 6:12* says spiritual wickedness in high places. This means you may be surprised where opposition rises up against you. It may come from people you would never expect it from. Secondly, you never have to fight an enemy with a weapon, your harsh words, or the silent treatment rather allow the

119

Lord to fight for you. Many times we feel if we allow the Lord to fight our battles we will be the weaker person. However, the bigger person NEVER tries to prove themselves. Many times our circle is too small for the level of success God wants to give us. How do you know when your circle is too small? Your circle is too small when you are the smartest one out the entire group. Or, when you are spiritual and the majority of your peers are carnal minded. Every time someone needs an answer they come to you. You can never find anyone in the group to give you any advice. I found out people who want to be the smartest, prettiest, or richest are very insecure. They hang out with people that have limitations so they can feel good about themselves. "***Iron sharpens Irons,***" mean that both parties are sharp. Your mentor should be able to learn something from you.

You cannot afford to be insecure because it will rob your greatness. You must understand what God has to say about you. So many times God believes in us more than we believe in ourselves. Jeremiah insisted that he could not be a prophet to the nation because he was too young. Moses believed that he could not be used by God because he did not have excellent speech. Esther believed that she could not speak to the king because during her time women were not to enter the King's chamber unless they were sent. So many people in the bible had limitations which made them feel insecure about their purpose. But, when we look to God we understand that his grace is sufficient and his strength is made perfect in our weaknesses.

Chapter 10

Seeing Your Life Support

I am afflicted very much: Revive me, O Lord, according to Your word.

Psalm 119:107 KJV

God's Word

Life support is often used in the medical industry when a patient is unable to maintain life after the failure of one or more vital organs. (found at http://medical-dictionary.thefreedictionary.com/life+support) It is often used as the last resource to help dying patients live. After experiencing those difficult situations in life, we often find ourselves depressed and exhausted with the chaos and turmoil of everyday living. During this stage, we need to totally depend on God's life support system which consists of God's word, Jesus, and other believers who have alike spirits. I often suggest that people read the word of God daily because it will change your life. For one, God's word is the truth therefore you can depend on it. It has accountability that if you obey it, you will receive its benefits. His word will give you insight on yourself and your situation. I strongly believe that a believer can not fight the good fight of faith if they are not enriched with the word of God. Sometimes when we experience hardship we feel no one understands but I guarantee you'll find someone you can relate to in the bible. I relate to King David because he shares the way he felt concerning his situations. David was an upright man but he was always honest with God. Sometimes I laugh at David's prayer for his enemies. He did not pray merciful prayers but vengeance prayers. Jesus told us to pray the merciful prayer for our enemies but David told the truth he wanted justice.   During the writing of this text, David had experienced many disappointments throughout the course of his life, yet he labored to be lively while serving God. He asked God in Psalm 119:107 to revive him which means to return to consciousness or life: become active or flourishing again. David knew that he had endured many things and God's word was his only comfort. Let's examine the condition of David's situations (1) Saul was a great and powerful enemy to David (2) David had fallen from God's grace by sleeping with Bathsheba and covering his sin by having Uriah (Bathsheba's husband) killed. (3) He lost a child through death. (4) Absalom his son tried to kill him. (5) Amnon his son raped his daughter Tamar. (6) At the writing of this particular scripture, David was sick and had reached old age. The situations he was facing many times left David distressed within his own soul. Many times David expressed the misery of his soul. He understood that some battles in life can actually knock the wind out of you. The pain is too heavy for us as humans. It can make you feel like death. After we have endured hardship for a long period of time, we sometimes can carry our troubling situations within our emotions. David probably had to endure damaged emotions like grief, loneliness, anger, resentment, guilt, and shame. These emotions if not taken to God can make even Christians give up. It is when you have been strong for others but you bear the burden of your own life situations. In this time of trouble, God's word is the only resource you can use. This phase of life support is only found in God's word. ***Uphold me according to Your word, that I may live; And do not let me be ashamed of my hope. Psalm 119:116*** At this point of his life, David can no longer depend on his strength to carry out his duty to God but the truth and holiness of God's word. He asked God to bring his word to manifestation that he will not be put to shame for having hope in his word. Life sometimes can be very dark but God's word will be a lamp for our feet that we may continually walk according to his will and a light into our path that we can stay on course with our purpose. If you are following the true person you are called to be you will have several obstacles. Purpose will not come easily. I chose to write this chapter after I told you that it is more to you than your current situations because to move to the next level it requires much work and depending on God's word than any other time. After reading God's word, you will have to put your faith into action. You will have to choose if you are going to fight with faith or let the enemy take you out. You want to live, then you must fight for it. I wanted success but I thought it was going to be easy. However, the more I desired to perform God's will for my life the more opposition I endured. I would receive prophesies (to foretell or predict) concerning a promising future but was unaware about the process. The woman with the issue of blood not only had a problem with her physical condition but she suffered emotionally, spiritually, and financially. She was socially isolated from the rest of the world due to her condition. It was a

123

disgrace for her to be in public. *And a woman was there who had been subject to bleeding for twelve years, but no one could heal her. She came up behind him and touched the edge of his cloak, and immediately her bleeding stopped. "Who touched me?" Jesus asked. When they all denied it, Peter said, "Master the people are crowding and pressing against you." But Jesus said, "Someone touched me; I know that power has gone out from me." Then the woman, seeing that she could not go unnoticed, came trembling and fell at his feet. In the presence of all the people, she told why she had touched him and how she had been instantly healed. Then he said to her, "Daughter, your faith has healed you. Go in peace." Luke 8: 43-48 NIV* This woman knew that her resources had ran out and she needed Jesus. She needed life support after 12 years of suffering she was probably exhausted from fighting for her healing. But, she yet pressed because Jesus is the word. *People who have suffered for years if not careful can become stagnated in their condition.* It was so hard for me to get out of my pit because I became comfortable with my current status. I couldn't see passed my situation. I would look into the mirror and see failure written across my face. But, God gave me life through His life support system. He sent people who imparted positive things into my life. *As iron sharpens iron, so one person sharpens another. Proverbs 27:17 NIV* It is so important that we have a vision for our lives that we surround ourselves around people who believes in our dreams. I once heard a preacher state that, "If you are the smartest person within your social circle you need to change friends". We sometimes prefer to be the smartest to make ourselves look intelligent. However, you are limiting yourself and not maximizing your full potential for growth. I felt as if I couldn't become a successful entrepreneur because within my previous social circle it was rare. People believed that being a young black single woman I was out of my mind. However, the more I read the bible the more I attracted people who followed their destinies.

Jesus Christ the Rest Giver

God's life support system is also used when everything else has failed. God should always be our first point of reference but sometimes we seek help outside of him. I imagine it is because we are humans and we think other humans seem to grant our requests faster. So, we reach out to other resources other than God. I know I did many times and every time I was disappointed. At this point in your journey, you should be exhausted from the battles that come to hinder our spiritual progress. God knows we become weary of our suffering sometimes. During this process, Jesus gave us one suggestion that many laborers in the body of Christ overlook. ***Come unto me, all ye that labor and are heavy laden, and I will give you rest. Matthew 11:28 KJV*** Many times evangelists, preachers, and teachers believe when we have reached a level in our ministries we shouldn't fall at the feet of Jesus ourselves. However, this scripture is referring to people who are laboring for Christ who are weary and the sinner. It can be applied to either person. There are people who are entangled in bondage and they are tired. You get tired of clubbing every weekend trying to find fulfillment. There are people who are tired of laboring for the Devil. *Sinners just need a way out*! Jesus often warned us that in this life we will have many tribulations and we should rejoice because then we are called blessed when we do. However, many times we lose sight on God's word about our situations and then we lose focus on who we are. The next verse Jesus tells readers to do ***"Take my yoke upon you, and learn of me; for I am meek and lowly in heart: and ye shall find rest unto your souls. Matthew 11:29KJV*** In order for us to learn of Jesus, we must read and mediate on God's word. LISTEN: BE CAREFUL NOT TO BE OVERLY CONCERNED WITH THIS WORLD. This is one of Satan's open doors. Worry! We worry about things that are temporary too much. You can not change anything in your life by worrying.

<u>Help My Mind</u>

Many people who confess to be Christians need to be revived in their minds. This revival I am speaking of can happen without inviting a guest evangelist to pray over you. I am speaking of seeing God's life support system among your troubles. A spiritual life support system is when God breathes on you again by sending a fresh anointing. Growing up in the Church of God in Christ I often heard stories how the older saints would pray and believe God to do supernatural miracles. But, I believe today's leaders need their own fresh wind from God. The fresh wind from God I am speaking of is the Holy Ghost. You can not operate this next assignment with the old anointing from when you first received Jesus. That's why we see so many dead ministries performing in the kingdom. They think the anointing from 1950 will cover this year. This next dimension requires you to depend on God as your only source. *It is when you realize it is not by might, nor by power, but by God's spirit. Zechariah 4:6* You can not depend on your own strength to complete God's assignment or you will fail. Attending Theological Seminary is a wise choice if you want to teach God's word, however if God does not give you the strength and wisdom the assignment will not be completed successfully.

It is not that we have done anything wrong but sometimes our battles in this world create spiritual exhaustion. We have done everything to get better but are not revived. Many people are serving in leadership who are spiritually burnt out. They constantly give out but never are poured into. That's why it's so important for us to stay within our lane. Everyone is not called in the pulpit some people are called in the audience to pray for the pulpit staff. Sometimes we are so busy with church work that we miss enjoying everyday life as Christians. When was the last time you were happy about serving Jesus? I've seen so many Christians without smiling or laughing, "I wonder God do they want to be saved"? Salvation shouldn't just be about obligations and duties but also enjoyment. I know we must suffer sometimes if we want to follow Christ however he came that we might live life to the fullest. (*John 10:10 KJV*) Jesus came to give life and I wonder if there is no life in people if he is in it. There are ministries that need to be resurrected. Sometimes they need to be resurrected because they are already dead. God never attended for us to walk around the world like zombies. We can not be a light if we are dead ourselves. I will be honest I reached a point in ministry where I was dead. I was tired of coming to church the way I came or feeling worst. I reached a defining moment with my walk with God. I was tired of being unproductive in ministry and I knew Jesus wasn't pleased because he wants us to bear fruit. (*John 15:2 KJV*) I had to be on life support for a while. That is when my spiritual walk behind close doors became more intense. I wanted more of Jesus not religion. I depended on God for everything. He feed me bread, gave me a new heart, cleansed my spirit, and prepared me for ministry. David said create in me a clean heart and renew within me a right spirit then I will teach transgressors your ways. (*Psalm 51:10 KJV*) *So many times people want to teach without having a heart transformation themselves.* I reached a point where I couldn't help people unless God helped me. They are people in ministry who are trying to help others publicly but privately they are struggling themselves. Yes, we all have struggles I'm not saying as leaders we are perfect. But, how can you give life to your followers if you are dead. That's like the blind leading the blind. We can not neglect our own personal souls trying to reach the lost. Jesus said there are people who are going to say ***Lord, Lord have I not done this in your name but he will say depart from me I know ye not. Matthew 7:21-23 KJV*** He does not know us because we never spend any quality time with him alone. Sometimes you have to get away by yourself and allow God to prepare and train you for the next dimension or you will miss it.

When the weary gets tired of waiting

I remember when a local pastor prophesied something I heard when I was twenty years old, ten years had passed by and the promise wasn't fulfilled. He told me I want you to praise God like it was your first time hearing it. I needed to be refreshed so many things had happened that made me doubt God was going to perform his word. God wants to bring life into your life. I know many things have happened to make you feel like your situation was all to you. But, it is still more to you than what people can see. Any day now God will make you live a life that will blow your mind. He is going to blow your mind. You have survived this far he is not going to fail you. Live! You do not have to die where you are. It would seem Jesus was unconcerned about healing Lazarus who was a close friend to him. *Jesus sent a word,* **"This sickness will not end in death. No, it is for God's glory so that God's glory so that God's Son may be glorified through it. "After Jesus sent his word, he continued to stay where he was while Lazarus grew worse. At Jesus' arrival Lazarus had been dead for four days. Lazarus' sister Martha was upset and told Jesus if you had been here Lazarus would be alive. Jesus told her your brother will rise again and Jesus performed a miracle by saying, "Lazarus, come forth." When Lazarus came forth he still was bound hand and foot by grave clothes Jesus demanded that the grave would loose and let him go. John 11:1-44** Sometimes all we need is a word that God is going to resurrect us again. God's word will bring life into any situation. Many times Jesus waits until our situation is dead before he comes to bring resurrection in our life so he can be glorified. He waits until the last friend betrays you and all your money is gone. I know what I'm talking about! Jesus will send us a word that he is coming but sometimes we look at our dead situation and doubt him. Some of us have been released from situations but like Lazarus we are still walking around with grave clothes. We still communicate to people God has told us to cut off. You want a release when the situation is discomforting but when they are satisfying us we are ok. Deliverance comes when it does not matter if the situation is discomforting or comforting we still want deliverance. Jesus wants to deliver you hand and foot. He wants to speak life back into every dead situation. One day I was driving and I heard the Holy Ghost say God wants to give you life again. As I pondered on what the Holy Ghost was saying, I thought about how God breathed life into Adam. *Genesis 2:7 And the LORD God formed man of the dust of the ground, and breathed into his nostrils the breath of life; and man became a living soul.* I started asking God to breathe into me again I needed to be resurrected from a dead spirit. I wanted God to breathe over my business, ministry, books, and every promise he agreed to do. I did not want to be just existing I wanted to have life and then produce into this world.

Give Me a New Heart

"I will give them an undivided heart and put a new spirit in them; I will remove from them their heart of stone and give them a heart of flesh." Ezekiel 11:19 NIV

130

The heart is the vital center and source of one's being, emotions, and sensibilities. I've noticed in the media people are always trying to fix their physical attributes they are insecure about. I rarely hear about celebrities having an extreme makeover in their spiritual journey. Many people in the church come to church with masks and do not examine the heart. Some transformations will not come overnight neither will it be easy. It will be a struggle and never allow anyone to make you feel bad about a struggle. I was a licensed Evangelist but I stayed on the altar both publically and privately. In Ezekiel 11:19, God says he will remove from them their heart of stone, this process is extremely painful. In the natural, doctors put you to sleep for a heart transplant because it is so painful and a high risk. God will remove things out of your life to give you a new heart. Removing things you are comfortable with will be painful. *No discipline seems pleasant at the time, but painful. Later on, however, it produces a harvest of righteousness and peace for those who have been trained by it. (Hebrews 12:11)* Change is painful. However, we must keep in mind that God is preparing us for a harvest of righteousness. In other words, the process is going to be rewarding especially when we go through the chastening. There are so many people that need to receive a heart transplant. You will be surprise how many people sit in churches with heart problems. I know because I was definitely one of them. They are consumed with hate, envy, unforgiveness, and other unproductive fruits. However, God began to heal me on the inside. Things and people I needed to let go I did. However, God began to reveal to me people I felt I could trust. I felt that these people related to

131

me and wouldn't judge me because I was dealing with issues we do not normally discuss within the four walls of the church. My biggest problem was I wrestled with unforgiveness. I would reminisce over negative words over and over in my head. I would have countless hours of sleepless nights because I couldn't heal over what was done to me.   Forgiveness does not help the other person but it helps you. Holding on to grudges will choke the very life out of you. I had to let it go. When I did it was so refreshing to my soul. I could no longer carry that weight of unforgiveness.

This new heart is needed for the next level of our journey. We can not take our excessive baggage into this new season. People often take their past experiences to new places and wonder why they have not experienced the life Jesus gives. We change jobs with the baggage of old jobs. We enter into new relationships with the same old memories from our previous relationships. When we do this we rob ourselves from enjoying the blessings of today. Transformation isn't based on our external state; rather it is based on the renewing of our minds. ***Do not conform to the pattern of this world, but be transformed by the renewing of your mind. Romans 12:2 NIV*** If an abusive woman hasn't transformed her mind after her first relationship then she will continue her patterns in future relationships. She will believe that being abused is a sign of love and find another man who looks different but still is an abusive person. However, if she reads her word daily, gives her life to Jesus, and changes her environment her mind will be transformed and she will refuse to be abused by anyone in the future. It is a true fact where our minds go our actions follow.

With this new heart we carry the fruit of the spirit which is love, joy, peace, forbearance, kindness, goodness, faithfulness, gentleness and self-control. These characteristics will make you feel like a brand new person. There are many people who serve in ministry that do not have these traits. However, having the fruit of the spirit places believers in a position to help someone else get delivered from their old self. God does not want to transform your life for your own enjoyment only. He wants to transform your life to help someone else. It is pointless for God to bless us with a new home, car, spouse, or ministry when we need a new heart. You still would be the same old person with better possessions. God wants to give us our desires as our soul matures he will grant our prayers. *Dear friend, I pray that you may enjoy good health and that all may go well with you, even as your soul is getting along well. 3 John 1:2*

Conclusion:

Seeing Yourself Getting Up

Rejoice not against me, O mine enemy: when I fall, I shall arise; when I sit in darkness, the Lord shall be a light unto me. Micah 7:8 KJV

The conclusion of the matter is: I got up! Dearly beloved I have opened up my heart and shared the most intimate testimonies in my life. I even had to relive some situations for you to walk into my shoes. The circumstances I shared in this book, I was unable to share within the four-walls of the church. The conclusion of the matter is I am more than a conqueror! God has delivered me from the enemy within me. I am currently working on rebuilding my life and enjoying the journey. I am an imaginary person therefore I picture myself in the recovery room after God has performed spiritual surgery on me. He has taken out bitterness, hatred, unforgiveness, and low self-worth out of me. I am waiting for ministry, business, and other people to break forth. I feel like busting loose! I may not be a New York Best Seller (Yet) but one thing I can tell you I have overcame the negative feelings about myself through the tactics of Satan! If you are looking at me through my past you are missing the miracle of God to change a person.

Since, the pain of yesterday God has worked on my life for the better. I started a new ministry and I am receiving so much word, joy, and love from my place of worship. God has blessed me with leaders not only who prepare me for heaven but they are teaching me how to live the abundant life on earth. They deal with real life issues that encourage me to confront the issues of my own life.

I started working at a new company which I love. I actually can't wait to go to work. That's weird but it's the truth. It's not only my income but it's my purpose. Each day as I go to the office I remember the days of struggling. The days were I had to stand in the unemployment lines. The days were I was a recipient of food stamps. The day I watched my entire life crumble apart. I can't help but praise and glorify God. I'm not ashamed of my struggle because I learned the most valuable lessons during my struggling days. I learned how to appreciate God through each step. Some people want you to believe that their degrees and social status helped them become successful. But, I can't give my degrees or social status any credit for God's goodness. I had two degrees which I graduated but still was underemployed. For a season, I worked a job which only paid $8.25 hourly. But, God was teaching me character. I would never despise my small days. Waking up at 4:30 am every morning to prepare for work taught me discipline.

As I did, I want you to CONFRONT AND DESTROY what has been trying to CONQUER you. Don't walk in fear! Don't allow your circumstances to cloud who God created you to be. For years I was silent, but you can refuse to be silent. It's so much more to you what people can see. They see inadequacy, failure, a castaway, or your past. God sees potential, greatness, success, and a conqueror. Let the King Arise in You! Refuse to feel sorry for yourself. Refuse to be a doormat to life and pick up the broken pieces. Refuse to be angry. Refuse to settle for less than your God given potential. My prayer is that you will become everything you were created to do not in man's eyes but in God's eyes. It's more to you than what we can see.

In Loving Memory Of Maya Angelou

You may write me down in history
With your bitter, twisted lies,
You may tread me in the very dirt
But still, like dust, I'll rise.

Does my sassiness upset you?
Why are you beset with gloom?
'Cause I walk like I've got oil wells
Pumping in my living room.

Just like moons and like suns,
With the certainty of tides,
Just like hopes springing high,
Still I'll rise.

Did you want to see me broken?
Bowed head and lowered eyes?
Shoulders falling down like teardrops.
Weakened by my soulful cries.

Does my haughtiness offend you?
Don't you take it awful hard
'Cause I laugh like I've got gold mines
Diggin' in my own back yard.

You may shoot me with your words,
You may cut me with your eyes,
You may kill me with your hatefulness.
But still, like air, I'll rise.

Out of the huts of history's shame
I rise
Up from a past that's rooted in pain
I rise
I'm a black ocean, leaping and wide,
Welling and swelling I bear in the tide.
Leaving behind nights of terror and fear
I rise
Into a daybreak that's wondrously clear
I rise
Bringing the gifts that my ancestors gave,
I am the dream and the hope of the slave.
I rise
I rise
I rise.

Scripture References

Scriptures on Attitude

Idolatry, participation in demonic activities, hostility, quarreling, jealousy, outbursts of anger, selfish ambition, divisions, the feeling that everyone is wrong except those in your own little group, envy, drunkenness, wild parties, and other kinds of sin. Let me tell you again, as I have before, that anyone living that sort of life will not inherit the Kingdom of God. But when the Holy Spirit controls our lives, he will produce this kind of fruit in us: love, joy, peace, patience, kindness, goodness, faithfulness, gentleness, and self-control. Here there is no conflict with the law. Galatians 5:20-23NLT

Don't be selfish; don't live to make a good impression on others. Be humble, thinking of others as better than yourself. Don't think only about your own affairs, but be interested in others, too, and what they are doing. Philippians 2:3-4 NLT

Finally, all of you should be of one mind, full of sympathy toward each other, loving one another with tender hearts and humble minds. 1 Peter 3:8

Since God chose you to be the holy people whom he loves, you must clothe yourselves with tenderhearted mercy, kindness, humility, gentleness, and patience. Colossians 3:12 NLT

Scriptures on Deliverance

Moses answered the people, "Do not be afraid. Stand firm and you will see the deliverance the LORD will bring you today. The Egyptians you see today you will never see again. Exodus 14:13 NIV

Then Hannah prayed and said: "My heart rejoices in the LORD; in the LORD my horn is lifted high. My mouth boasts over my enemies, for I delight in your deliverance. I Samuel 2:1 NIV

Then they cried out to the LORD in their trouble, and he delivered them from their distress. Psalm 107:6 NIV

The righteous cry out, and the LORD hears them; he delivers them from all their troubles. Psalm 34:17 NIV

And he said, the LORD is my rock, and my fortress, and my deliverer; 2 Samuel 22:2 KJV

But the LORD said unto me, Say not, I am a child: for thou shalt go to all that I shall send thee, and whatsoever I command thee thou shalt speak. Be not afraid of their faces: for I am with thee to deliver thee, saith the LORD. Jeremiah 1:7-8 KJV

For sin shall not be your master, because you are not under law, but under grace. What then? Shall we sin because we are not under law but under grace? By no means! Don't you know that when you offer yourselves to someone to obey him as slaves, you are slaves to the one whom you obey whether you are slaves to sin, which leads to death, or to obedience, which leads to righteousness. But thanks be to God that, though you used to be slaves to sin, you wholeheartedly obeyed the form of teaching to which you were entrusted. You have been set free from sin and have become slaves to righteousness. Romans 6:14-18 NIV

Scriptures on Depression

And Nehemiah continued, "Go and celebrate with a feast of choice foods and sweet drinks, and share gifts of food with people who have nothing prepared. This is a sacred day before our Lord. Don't be dejected and sad, for the joy of the LORD is your strength!" Nehemiah 8:10 NLT

Finally, brothers, whatever is true, whatever is noble, whatever is right, whatever is pure, whatever is lovely, whatever is admirable if anything is excellent or praiseworthy think about such things. Philippians 4:8 NIV

And we know that all things work together for good to them that love God, to them who are the called according to his purpose. Romans 8:28 KJV

"Come to me, all you who are weary and burdened, and I will give you rest. Take my yoke upon you and learn from me, for I am gentle and humble in heart, and you will find rest for your souls. For my yoke is easy and my burden is light." Matthew 11:28-30 NIV

Cast all your anxiety on him because he cares for you. I Peter 5:7 NIV

So do not fear, for I am with you; do not be dismayed, for I am your God. I will strengthen you and help you; I will uphold you with my righteous right hand. Isaiah 41:10 NIV

Scriptures on Overcoming Failure

The LORD upholds all those who fall and lifts up all who are bowed down. Psalm 145:14 NIV

For though a righteous man falls seven times, he rises again, but the wicked are brought down by calamity. Proverbs 24:16 NIV

Rejoice not against me, O mine enemy: when I fall, I shall arise; when I sit in darkness, the LORD shall be a light unto me. Micah 7:8 KJV

For we do not have a high priest who is unable to sympathize with our weaknesses, but we have one who has been tempted in every way, just as we are yet was without sin. Let us then approach the throne of grace with confidence, so that we may receive mercy and find grace to help us in our time of need. Hebrews 4:15-16 NIV

David also said to Solomon his son, "Be strong and courageous, and do the work. Do not be afraid or discouraged, for the LORD God, my God, is with you. He will not fail you or forsake you until all the work for the service of the temple of the LORD is finished. I Chronicles 28:20 NIV

When you pass through the waters, I will be with you; and when you pass through the rivers, they will not sweep over you. When you walk through the fire, you will not be burned; the flames will not set you ablaze. For I am the LORD, your God, the Holy One of Israel, your Savior; Isaiah 43;2-3

Scriptures on Healing

But he was wounded for our transgressions, he was bruised for our iniquities: the chastisements of our peace was upon him; and with his stripes we are healed. Isaiah 53:5 KJV

When the even was come, they brought unto him many that were possessed with devils: and he cast out the spirits with his word, and healed all that were sick: Matthew 8:16 KJV

But when Jesus knew it, he withdrew himself from thence: and great multitudes followed him, and he healed them all; Matthew 12:15 KJV

Then was brought unto him one possessed with a devil, blind, and dumb: and he healed him, insomuch that the blind and dumb both spake and saw. Matthew 12:22 KJV

And Jesus went forth, and saw a great multitude, and was moved with compassion toward them, and he healed their sick Matthew 14:14 KJV

Large crowds followed him, and he healed them there. Matthew 19:2 NIV

Scriptures on Visions

For the vision is yet for an appointed time, but at the end it shall speak, and not lie: though it tarry, wait for it; because it will surely come, it will not tarry. Habakkuk 2:3KJV

Where there is no vision, the people perish: but he that keepeth the law, happy is he. Proverbs 29:18 KJV

Scriptures on Prosperity

But remember the LORD your God, for it is he who gives you the ability to produce wealth, and so confirms his covenant, which he swore to your ancestors, as it is today. Deuteronomy 8:18 NIV

Beloved, I wish above all things that thou mayest prosper and be in health, even as thy soul prospereth. 3 John 1:2 KJV

Trust in the LORD and do good; dwell in the land and enjoy safe pasture. Delight yourself in the LORD and he will give you the desires of your heart. Psalm 37:3-4 NIV

Bring ye all the tithes into the storehouse, that there may be meat in mine house, and prove me now herewith, saith the LORD of hosts, if I will not open you the windows of heaven, and pour you out a blessing, that there shall not be room enough to receive it. Malachi 3:10 KJV

For I know the plans I have for you, "declares the LORD, "plans to prosper you and not to harm you, plans to give you hope and a future. Jeremiah 29:11 NIV

Scriptures of Overcoming Insecurity

For the LORD your God has arrived to live among you. He is a mighty savior. He will rejoice over you with great gladness. With his love, he will calm all your fears. He will exult over you by singing a happy song." Zephaniah 3:17 NLT

But the Lord is faithful; he will make you strong and guard you from the evil one. 2 Thessalonians 3:3 NLT

Those who live in the shelter of the Most High will find rest in the shadow of the Almighty. This I declare of the LORD: He alone is my refuge, my place of safety; he is my God, and I am trusting in him. For he will rescue you from every trap and protect you from the fatal plague. He will shield you with his wings. He will shelter you with his feathers. His faithful promises are your armor and protection. Do not be afraid of the terrors of the night, nor fear the dangers of the day, nor dread the plague that stalks in darkness, nor the disaster that strikes at midday. Though a thousand fall at your side, though ten thousand are dying around you, these evils will not touch you. Psalm 91:1-7 NLT

We are confident of all this because of our great trust in God through Christ. It is not that we think we can do anything of lasting value by ourselves. Our only power and success come from God. He is the one who has enabled us to represent his new covenant. 2 Corinthians 3:4-6 NLT

"So I tell you, don't worry about everyday life whether you have enough food, drink, and clothes. Doesn't life consist of more than food and clothing? Look at the birds. They don't need to plant or harvest or put food in barns because your heavenly Father feeds them. And you are far more valuable to him than they are. Can all your worries add a single moment to your life? Of course not. And why worry about your clothes? Look at the lilies and how they grow. They don't work or make their clothing, yet Solomon in all his glory was not dressed as beautifully as they are. And if God cares so wonderfully for flowers that are here today and gone tomorrow, won't he more surely care for you? You have so little faith! So don't worry about having enough food or drinks or clothing. Why be like the pagans who are so deeply concerned about these things? Your heavenly Father already knows all your needs, and he will give you all you need from day to day if you live for him and make the Kingdom of God your primary concern. So don't worry about tomorrow, for tomorrow will bring its own worries. Today's trouble is enough for today. Matthew 6:25-34

Scriptures on Being Comfortable With Ourselves

Don't copy the behavior and customs of this world, but let God transform you into a new person by changing the way you think. Then you will know what God wants you to do, and you will know how good and pleasing and perfect his will really is. Romans 12:2 NLT

Don't let anyone think less of you because you are young. Be an example to all believers in what you teach, in the way you live, in your love, your faith, and your purity. I Timothy 4:12 NLT

See how very much our heavenly Father loves us, for he allows us to be called his children, and we really are! But the people who belong to this world don't know God, so they don't understand that we are his children. I John 3:1 NLT

And I am sure that God, who began the good work within you, will continue his work until it is finally finished on that day when Christ Jesus comes back again. Philippians 1:6 NLT

Therefore I, a prisoner for serving the Lord, beg you to lead a life worthy of your calling, for you have been called by God. Be humble and gentile. Be patient with each other, making allowance for each other's faults because of your love. Ephesians 4:1-2 NLT

A Letter from Tequila

Dear Reading Audience,

I would like to personally thank you for sharing your time in my first book. I appreciate and love you very much.

This book wasn't designed to destroy or put anyone down. The stories I share were real life moments that defined my life. I love and forgive everyone. I ask for everyone forgiveness that I offended.

I pray and ask God to command a special blessing on your life. I pray that God gives you abundant favor in every area of your life.

If you'd like to share your thoughts about "It's More to Me Than What You See", feel free to contact me via email, web, or facebook.

I hope you become courageous and share your story!!! It's more to YOU than what people can see.

In God's Love,

Tequila L. Carter

If you have any questions or testimonials please send to:
 itsmore2me@outlook.com (email)
www.itsmore2me.vpweb.com (web)
Tequilla Carter (facebook)

Tequila Lasandra Carter, is a modern-day woman description of David, a woman after God's own heart. She dedicated her life to Christ at the age 15 at a New Year's Revival conducted by Evangelist Barbara Jackson-Sago. At the age sixteen, she received the baptism of the Holy Ghost. Due to her dedication to God, her challenges in life begin at an early age. She has served in many capacities within the church Y.P.W.W. Chairlady for the A.B. McEwen District where she encouraged the young people to live a saved and balanced life. She holds a Bachelor's degree in Business Administration. By profession, she works in the retail industry and an entrepreneur. She is the founder and owner of Tequila's Secret Closet a jewelry retail company for women. She has an overcoming testimony to share to the world. She plans to donate copies of her new book to the Shelby County Prison Library. She believes in being a transparent leader to help people overcome their personal challenges. Her greatest ambition in life is to serve God and his people with compassion, humility, integrity, and excellence.